BECOMING
THE CHANGE

BECOMING THE CHANGE

THE POWER OF CULTURAL INTELLIGENCE

LOREN ROSARIO-MALDONADO

MANUSCRIPTS
PRESS

BECOMING THE CHANGE
The Power of Cultural Intelligence

ISBN   979-8-88926-546-7 *Paperback*
           979-8-88926-547-4 *Ebook*

Contents

Foreword

———

Foreword for *Becoming the Change: The Power of Cultural Intelligence*

I've been waiting for a book like this one to be written—one that presents ideas rooted in the academically rigorous research of cultural intelligence but brought to life through the author's lived experience. Usually, we get one or the other. But you're about to read one that seamlessly weaves together rigorous, academically rich insights with the lived reality of a vibrant, multicultural, culturally intelligent woman.

I've spent twenty-five years researching, writing, and teaching cultural intelligence. That sounds like the kind of thing a guy named "David Livermore" would do, right? But I need people like Loren Rosario-Maldonado who help me see what cultural intelligence looks like in the real world. I mean, just stop and think about the difference in our names for a second. Loren. Rosario. Maldonado. If that isn't enough to intrigue you, her experience as a Dominican woman growing up in the boroughs of New York City most certainly will. But that's only one part of her identity. She has a long-time career in HR and business. She's a nerdy academic who loves exploring the depths of neuroscience, psychology, and cultural intelligence. And she's a devoted spouse, mother, aunt, mentor, and lover of people anywhere life takes her. I've seen it firsthand.

Loren, like so many of us, is quintessentially her nationality while at the same time not very typical Dominican or American. And that comes through in how she's written *Becoming the Change.* She provides us with guideposts for what to expect when interacting with people in light of their cultural identities. But she also gives us tools to help ensure we don't put people in boxes.

Whether you're a business leader trying to improve the way you do DEI, an individual trying to figure out where you land on the diversity spectrum, or someone on the quest to make sense of your own identity, this book is your guide. It shows you how to use the power of cultural intelligence to be the change.

Loren's life and book are an invitation to all of us to more fully become ourselves while allowing others to do the same. And together, we will build a more culturally intelligent world, one interaction at a time.

David Livermore, PhD
Boston University

Preface

Knowing yourself is the beginning of all wisdom.
—*ARISTOTLE*

"Is there a particular reason why you always speak in Spanish?" I recall asking an employee in our weekly one-on-one. I still cringe at this memory. As a high achiever, I assumed that others' sense of achievement was like mine, and I approached my leadership style the same way, through the lens of achievement. I was trying to boost and polish her professionally by urging her to practice her English more. Although I had the best intentions, the insensitivity behind my conversation was not motivational, and our relationship was doomed from the start. This conversation was one of our first encounters since I started working with her. Little did I know it would be the one that would set the tone for our future relationship. I didn't see this as an opportunity to build trust and rapport with her because I was so focused on achievement that I missed this critical social cue. The weight of my mistake hung heavily over me as I struggled to make amends over time. Another cultural faux pas on my part!

THE SHIFT

This is a story of self-discovery. You see, I lived much of my life under the influence of cultural assumptions that, unbeknownst to me, were shaping my actions and interactions, both in my personal life and career.

Allow me to take you back to a pivotal moment in my life, five years ago, when I stepped into a multicultural counseling class during my master's program. The objective was clear: understanding cultural differences and their history and developing the skills required to counsel diverse communities. I was eager and ready to learn how to guide various populations, knowing that, as a global leader, my understanding needed to expand beyond my somewhat sheltered, middle-class female perspective.

My journey up until that point had been relatively smooth. I had a comfortable upbringing, a quality education, and ample opportunities for success. I was blissfully unaware of the structural forces that propelled my life in certain directions until I was confronted with the profound concept of "unearned societal privilege" based on my skin color.

The class thesis required an in-depth immersion into a culture of our choosing to comprehend its history and societal norms. I chose to delve into my own Dominican culture, an area I needed to gain more knowledge of outside of platanos (fried plantains), queso frito (fried cheese), and Merengue (our national dance).

As I delved deeper into my coursework, I was stunned. Case studies and sociological data highlighted the systemic inequalities and privileges I had been oblivious to for so long. This revelation of privilege, this jarring reality check, threw my identity into question. After all, I had always believed in meritocracy, or the power of hard work leading to success. To realize that my achievements weren't solely the product of my efforts but were, in part, due to systemic advantages was humbling, even shocking.

The more I disconnected from my fragmented identity, the more I found myself in an existential crisis, unsure of my affiliations, who I was, and where I came from. The culture of my heritage and my culturally neutral self clashed, creating a fissure in my self-perception. I was taken aback to realize my skin color had bestowed upon me unearned privileges, making me, to my horror, complicit in microaggressive acts and, yes, even racism.

Despite having service as a central tenet of my moral code, I lived in a culturally agnostic state that, while adaptable and valuable, masked my privilege. My ignorance of this privilege led me to inadvertently disrespect others' cultural values and identities. I grappled with a fragmented identity that persists today as I took a deep and brutally honest look at all the parts of me that influenced my life and those I served.

Standing on the precipice of a cultural divide, I was confronted with the profound disconnect between my identity, cultural values, and Dominican roots. It was a daunting revelation: My existence was teetering on the edge of a cultural abyss, a void widened by years of acting as a cultural chameleon.

That my oversight of the integral aspects of someone's identity could be a subtle form of discrimination was a bitter pill to swallow. I found myself feeling guilty for participating in minor behaviors that had the potential to harm people. This realization left me feeling regretful, guilty, and conflicted. And I was not alone. I realized I was unknowingly perpetuating behaviors that had persisted for generations, even as a global HR leader.

But amid this whirlwind of self-discovery and introspection, I discovered Cultural Intelligence (CQ). This framework gave me the tools to appreciate, understand, and adapt to different cultures, including my own. It taught me that our differences are not barriers but bridges if we allow them to be. Embracing my cultural intelligence, I began understanding how my cultural values shaped my lived experience. I learned my identity is multidimensional and shaped by those lived experiences, which were determined by my cultural values. This tumultuous existential crisis was no longer a burden but an opportunity to see the world through a multitude of lenses and to appreciate the richness of diversity.

PRIVILEGE

As the child of a middle-class Christian preacher, I was raised with the values of service, morality, and seeing goodness in others. It's the upbringing that paints a picture of hope and aspiration. But, like many things in life, my understanding of the world was not without its flaws. I used to see privilege through a particular lens—wealth and societal power with the assumption that it was as simple as that. If you had money and held sway in society, you were privileged. But I realize this view is far too narrow and disconnected from the rich tapestry of human experience.

Recognizing my privileges in certain areas is a humbling experience. Privilege isn't something we often think consciously about. Privilege is not just about the size of your bank account or societal influence. It is qualitative as much as it is quantitative. It's interwoven with the cultural identities we carry and the personal journeys we undertake. Especially if we benefit from it, it's like an invisible tailwind that propels us forward and can be related to various aspects of our identity, such as race, gender, class, or geographical location.

Imagine walking into a room filled with a buffet of experiences. Now, picture your choices based on your preferences and what you seek, shaping your unique taste. That's what forming our identity is like—a complex blend of our choices, circumstances, and, importantly, cultural values and privilege.

Let's start by looking at cultural values. They're like the recipes passed down through generations, forming a roadmap for our behaviors, beliefs, and even our approach to life. We interpret the world and our place within it through this cultural lens. It's like being in a dance where our upbringing and societal norms have influenced the music, rhythm, and steps.

But here's the twist: While we're all participating in this dance, only some hear the same music or move to the same beat. That's where privilege comes in, a dimension of our lives that often goes unnoticed, particularly by those who possess it.

Imagine privilege as an all-access pass you've somehow ended up with. It grants an unobstructed view of the stage and a smoother dance floor to twirl on. This pass isn't something you've asked for, nor is it something you've necessarily earned. It's based on aspects of your identity that society values more, maybe your race, class, gender, or sexual orientation.

Cultural values and privilege aren't operating in silos. They're intricately woven, influencing our sense of identity. Suppose you've been raised in a culture valuing independence and self-expression and have been lucky enough to have the privilege. In that case, your dance moves will likely be confident and unapologetic. Your world is your stage, and your identity develops with a stronger sense of self-assured individuality.

Now, consider another scenario. You're from a culture where collective harmony and respect for authority are paramount. But let's say your all-access pass has some limitations. You're marginalized due to factors beyond your control—socioeconomic background, education, race, or gender. This scenario throws in unique choreography. While your cultural values lean toward community and shared experiences, the hurdles you face may inculcate resilience and an awareness of systemic inequalities, contributing to a more complex, multifaceted identity.

Once I began acknowledging privilege, I realized it doesn't define me completely. So yes, I am privileged, but that's not where my story ends. It's an essential puzzle piece chapter in my book, but only part of the picture. That's where cultural values come into play. These principles, norms, and beliefs have been instilled in me since childhood. They're shaped by my family, community, and country, forming the core of who I am.

My identity is shaped by many things, from the cultural values ingrained in me to the experiences I've had, the people I've met, the lessons I've learned, and the privileges I've been granted.

UNDERSTANDING MY ROOTS

Let's talk honestly about culture, privilege, and how our early experiences shape our perceptions of the world. Sometimes, we can live with blinders, only seeing what's directly in front of us, failing to realize that we are part of a vast, intricate tapestry of culture and history. And I was no exception. For so long, I was disconnected from my cultural roots, which shaped my perspective of life.

I was born and raised in the United States to Dominican immigrants. My parents instilled a strong sense of familial duty, collective responsibility, and interdependence. In their culture, prioritizing family above all else, including one's aspirations, was a deeply held value.

I lived in predominantly Anglo neighborhoods and attended local schools. From an early age, I was steeped in mainstream American society's cultural norms and values. The emphasis on individualism, independence, and direct communication shaped my worldview. From an early age, I absorbed the societal values around me, shaped by the predominant Anglo-American culture in my community. The American ideals of independence, personal achievement, and autonomy shaped my outlook on life.

At the same time, my home was a slice of the Dominican Republic in America, with its bustling relationships, the tantalizing aroma of traditional dishes, and the Spanish language filling the air. My parents held tight to their cultural values, including a strong sense of family, respect for elders, collectivism, shared responsibility, and a more indirect approach to communication. Although I spoke English fluently, I could not speak it at home. As I grew older, I found myself caught between these two worlds. At school, assertiveness and outspokenness were praised, reflecting the valued traits in American culture. But at home, these qualities were considered offensive and disrespectful, particularly toward elders.

As I grew older, the tension between my American and Dominican values became more pronounced. I was thrilled when I received an offer in my senior year of high school to attend college away from home. It wasn't very far, and I could not resist the opportunity. But my mom had different expectations. In addition to the cost, she believed I should attend a local college to remain close to home and continue to play an active role in family life, helping care for my younger sister.

My American upbringing taught me to seize the opportunity for higher education and personal growth, viewing it as a step toward independence and success. Yet, my family's concerns were rooted in Dominican values emphasizing family cohesion, collective support, and shared responsibility.

Caught between these contrasting cultural values, I faced a tough decision. On the one hand, I was eager to forge my path, consistent with the individualistic values I adapted from the broader American society. On the other hand, I felt a strong sense of obligation to my family and collectivist Dominican roots. Ultimately, I chose to stay home and attend a local college.

My story highlights a few complexities of balancing differing cultural values at home. Many individuals, primarily second-generation immigrants, face navigating different cultural value systems within their families. Balancing the pursuit of personal aspirations with familial responsibilities can be a delicate task, requiring communication, understanding, and, sometimes, difficult compromises.

In this bubble I created for myself, I was continuously striving to do better, to be better, failing to acknowledge the privileges I already had. But then came a turning point. And let me tell you, it changed everything.

A CALL TO ACTION

And thus, the road to my metamorphosis unfurled before me. I faced my shame and stared it down with a resilience born from newfound understanding. As I embarked on this enlightening journey, it was not just about learning but also unlearning—a task just as crucial. I scrutinized and questioned the biases and microaggressions I had unknowingly participated in. And I made a choice. I made a bold **C.H.O.I.C.E.** to become the change.

C—I summoned the courage to accept my journey and radically accept my biases in my search for self-awareness.

H—I humbled myself to the idea that bias is a part of me and all of us, and differences do not divide us. They unite us.

O—I became open to new experiences. I sought mentors and engaged in meaningful conversations with people from diverse backgrounds to gain different perspectives.

I—I Integrated what I was learning with action each step of the way.

C—I became curious about our cultural differences and how they impact our behavior.

E—I summoned empathy for myself and others in this learning journey. I educated myself about my cultural values and how they impact my personal and professional relationships.

Believe me when I tell you my path was not without its tribulations. As I deepened my understanding of cultural values, a storm of confusion and discomfort often cast a shadow over me. Yet, I embraced these moments' pivotal role in molding my evolution. As an Afro-Latina who identifies as white, self-discovery was not just about understanding my cultural values or privileges. It was about confronting and dismantling the biases I carried within me. This was a critical step. It wasn't just about paving the way for a society brimming with inclusivity and equity but also about making room within myself for that inclusivity and equity to flourish.

I wanted to help cultivate a community where individuals, regardless of skin color, could celebrate their unique identities without the specter of discrimination or marginalization looming over them. To do that, I had to face my biases and understand how they were a byproduct of my cultural values and privilege.

I had to grapple with the reality that my cultural values were only sometimes shared or universally beneficial. Understanding this fusion of cultural values and privilege didn't weaken my identity; it strengthened it. I realized my identity is multidimensional, composed of my heritage, my beliefs, my experiences, and, yes, my privileges.

This combined to form a unique blend that is constantly evolving as I learn and grow. The dance of identity formation is an ongoing process, an intricate tango of understanding and accepting the multifaceted nature of who I am. It's about navigating the complex interplay between cultural values, privilege, and personal biases.

It's a rich, challenging journey, but one that's worth every step. Because, at the end of the day, recognizing and embracing the complexity of our identities allows us to engage more authentically and empathetically with the world around us. And that is a step toward the inclusive and equitable society we all envision.

I had to exit the comfortable sphere I knew and come face-to-face with my biases. There were moments cloaked in vulnerability, enveloped in self-doubt, and tinged with discomfort. Yet, through this transformative process, I came to celebrate the unique beauty of my fragmented cultural identity and the significance of understanding and appreciating the diverse identities around me.

And my transformation didn't halt with my evolution. As I continued to grow, I recognized the capacity I had to set in motion a wave of change, to ignite a spark in others, prompting them to embark on their journeys of self-discovery and understanding. I became a fervent champion of cultural intelligence within my circle.

Today, I wear my journey of transformation as a badge of honor. It has shaped a life that resonates with meaning, influence, and change. Cultivating cultural intelligence has gifted me joy, allowing me to make peace with my fragmented identity and foster a more interconnected and unified world through CQ.

So, as I unravel the tapestry of my and others' stories before you, I invite you to embark on this journey alongside me. Not to alter who you are or what you believe but to open your eyes to the power of cultural intelligence, learn about your cultural preferences, question your biases, and revel in the beauty of human diversity.

Let's forge ahead, creating a world where everyone feels seen, heard, and cherished.

Introduction

———

Knowing others is intelligence; knowing yourself is true wisdom.
—*LAO TZU*

"Holy shit! I'm Black!" I cried.

"Duh, you're the only one who doesn't realize that," my sister tells me.

As I scanned my 23andMe results, I noticed that my ancestry is 50 percent African, starkly contrasting the Dominican ancestry I identified with. I was quickly learning that being Dominican represented a diaspora of different cultures.

LOOKING WITHIN

And there I was, standing at a crossroads amid an identity crisis, stirred up by a profound period of self-reflection and growth. It was a moment that had me questioning the essence of who I was, who I believed myself to be, and, most importantly, who I aspired to become. You see, what had begun as a crisis was, in fact, a catalyst, making me more sensitive, more empathetic, and, more importantly, pushing me into action to challenge the systemic inequities that surround us.

I found myself on a journey—a constant ebb and flow of unlearning what I thought I knew and soaking up new perspectives. And here's the revelation that I came to: This process isn't about shedding my identity. It's about transforming and evolving into a more informed, compassionate, and proactive version of myself.

This evolution is our road map to a more just society. The path might be winding or steep, but it leads us forward. As I set foot on the journey toward discovering cultural values, I found myself drawn to the wisdom of cultural intelligence (Earley and Ang 2003, 29). I realized that understanding cultural values, which guide our chosen paths in life, is a key aspect of cultivating cultural intelligence (Livermore 2009, 13). These values profoundly influence our communication, work, approach to conflict, and even how we eat and perceive time. Initially, I believed my cultural preferences were based on a binary of good and bad. However, cultural intelligence opened my eyes to a new perspective. These values are not about right or wrong. They're about the unique ways we navigate life (Livermore 2011, 102).

In my deep dive into cultural intelligence, or CQ, I immersed myself in a vibrant, intricate tapestry of diverse threads. You see, every facet of our identity, every unique experience, plays a role in shaping this beautiful and complex mosaic of diversity (Livermore 2009, 122). As I became more sensitive to these cultural nuances, I began seeing the world through a kaleidoscopic lens, each piece symbolizing an intricate story.

CULTURAL TAPESTRY

In the diverse mosaic of our global community, a myriad of cultural values and beliefs weave together, forming a beautiful canvas of shared humanity. Yet, within this vibrant tapestry, potential conflicts lie hidden, born from the unique differences that set us apart. As we steer our way through this complex landscape, the variations in our communication styles, work ethics, and decision-making processes can lead to misunderstandings, causing ripples in our relationships with others.

The intricate balance between individualism and collectivism, the complex layers of gender roles, our orientation toward time, and even our religious beliefs add depth to our interactions. These differences can sometimes stir up conflicts that undermine our strive for harmony. Even our perspectives on uncertainty and the unspoken rules that govern our daily lives can create discord.

However, we find growth, understanding, and unity opportunities within this diverse panorama (Livermore 2011, 13). As we learn to appreciate and navigate the spectrum of cultural values, we build stronger bonds with others and discover the hidden beauty and wisdom in our global tapestry.

However, areas where a cultural values mismatch can complicate matters and escalate the potential for conflict. Some of the most common ones include:

Communication: Misunderstandings stemming from differences in language, nonverbal cues, or communication styles can lead to confusion and conflict.

Value and belief systems: Differences in social norms, ethics, religious practices, or cultural values can create tension and disagreements.

Decision-making: Cultural variances can affect our approach to problem-solving, decision-making, and negotiation, leading to potential misunderstandings, particularly in professional settings.

Workplace dynamics: Different expectations around hierarchy, power dynamics, management styles, and teamwork can shape workplace interactions.

Stereotyping and bias: Cultural differences can sometimes fuel stereotypes, prejudice, or discrimination, harming relationships and creating divisions.

Work-life balance: Different cultural views on balancing work and personal life can lead to conflicts or misunderstandings in personal and professional scenarios.

Customer expectations: Variances in cultural expectations about customer service, product preferences, or marketing strategies can influence a company's success across different markets.

Negotiation styles: Cultural influences can affect negotiation tactics and outcomes, potentially impacting business relationships and agreements.

Time orientation: Differences in the perception and value of time can lead to mismatched expectations, impacting punctuality and deadlines.

Rituals and traditions: Variances in cultural rituals, ceremonies, or traditions can present challenges when coordinating efforts or planning events among diverse groups.

Emotional expression: Variations in emotional expression and regulation across cultures can affect our ability to connect with others on an emotional level.

Trust building: Misunderstandings across all value dimensions, such as uncertainty orientation, affect our ability to build trust by creating perceived insensitivity in our actions.

BECOMING

Now, let's be honest here. I've always been the kind of person who loves meeting new people and getting to know their stories. But back then, I was on the outskirts looking in, my gaze clouded by the stereotypes and preconceived notions that media often perpetuates.

However, my journey into CQ started peeling back those layers, uncovering realities that far surpassed the surface-level perceptions I once held. I discovered, for instance, how time—something so universal—is viewed differently across cultures. I knew time was linear, measured, and compartmentalized in the world—a commodity to be bought and spent. But delving deeper into the heart of CQ, I understood that, for some cultures, time is a fluid concept, a cyclic rhythm woven into the tapestry of life.

Then, there was the revelation about relationships. Coming from a culture where individuality is held on a pedestal, interdependence was a novel concept. I started to see communities where the collective trumps the individual, where relationships are built and nurtured on a foundation of trust and mutual respect above all else, meant to endure through time.

Conflict, too, emerged in different hues on this journey. What I had grown to associate with negativity, I found, was seen as a conduit for growth and relationship building in some cultures, while in others, it was a thing to be sidestepped for the sake of collective harmony.

Even silence spoke volumes, I found. Where I came from, silence is a void to be filled, an uncomfortable absence. But, in other cultures, silence is a mark of respect, a testament to thoughtful consideration. I began to appreciate these quiet moments and understand their cultural significance.

And let's not forget communication—the very essence of human interaction. In my direct, no-beat-around-the-bush culture, I discovered I was seen as cold and distant by those from cultures where communication is indirect and implicit. By tempering my directness with subtlety, I found a middle ground, enhancing my ability to communicate across cultural lines.

The concept of power distance was an eye-opener too. My culture celebrates a democratic leadership style, encouraging open discussions and challenging the status quo. But I witnessed cultures that respect the power hierarchy, where those at the top make decisions, and dissent is not welcomed. In these environments, I had to adapt, shifting my leadership style to maintain harmony within the group.

Each day, I found myself deeper in understanding this cultural tapestry. It honed my patience, my consideration, and my understanding. I became a better listener, not just to the spoken word but to the silences in between. I realized our backgrounds and cultural experiences form an integral part of us, shaping who we are. To appreciate these differences and their unifying power is the essence of cultural intelligence.

Sure, there were moments of discomfort, times when I stumbled or inadvertently caused offense. But I saw each of these instances as opportunities to learn and grow. My identity crisis hasn't entirely passed. There's still confusion, frustration, and guilt. But I've seen these discomforts are essential to dismantling long-held beliefs and societal structures. I'm grateful for this journey and the wisdom it has imparted, and I am eager to keep evolving, learning, and growing on this path.

So, as we come to the close of this chapter, let's pause and reflect. Recognizing these conflict zones is not about staking out divisions or drawing lines in the sand but has the potential to be far more enlightening than that. It's not about stereotyping but understanding ourselves and others (Livermore 2011, 102).

You see, it's about deepening our understanding of one another, about peeling back the layers of our shared human experience to reveal the radiant core beneath. It's about acknowledging and, yes, even celebrating our differences, not as stumbling blocks but as the beautiful stepping stones they truly are—bridges that guide us to the rich oasis of harmony amid the lush diversity that defines our world.

Each of these experiences, each cultural nuance, each unique perspective, weaves a single, vibrant thread. And when woven together, these threads form the radiant, colorful tapestry of our shared global community. Each thread is crucial and cherished, adding its unique hue to our shared masterpiece.

More than just understanding for the sake of understanding, this is about finding unity in our diversity, about creating a symphony from the myriad notes that each culture brings to the grand orchestra of life. It's about standing together, hand in hand, under the vast sky of our shared human experience and recognizing the truth—that our differences don't divide but unite us.

The picture that emerges is more than just vibrant or colorful. It's nothing short of wondrous, a true testament to the extraordinary power of diversity. So, as we end this chapter and prepare for the next, let's hold on to that vision. Because, my friends, that's the power of understanding. That's the beauty of diversity. And that, truly, is the miracle of our shared human journey.

With that thought, let's turn the page… The next chapter awaits!

PART 1

WHAT GOT US HERE

CHAPTER 1

Who Are *You?*

———

*To be yourself in a world that is constantly trying to make
you something else is the greatest accomplishment.*
—RALPH WALDO EMERSON

"Where are you from?" asks the person.

"I'm from New York," I reply.

"No, where are you really from? You don't sound like a New
Yorker," was the reply.

I get this question often, and honestly, I don't know how
to respond half the time. Am I a New Yorker? Am I Afro-
Latina? Am I Dominican? A wife? A mother? A daughter?
All of the above.

WHO ARE *YOU?*

Have you ever wondered why we think and feel the way we do? Our identity comprises countless dimensions: ethnicity, gender, socioeconomic status, religion, neurodiversity, and age. Each of these shapes us, molding us into unique individuals.

Now, imagine that each of these identity pieces is a color. We're not just a plain white canvas but vibrant paintings with diverse colors blending. That's where cultural values come in—they're the palette from which these colors are drawn. Cultural values are those principles and standards that shape our actions, thoughts, and feelings. Often so deep-seated that we're unaware of them, they dictate what we see as right or wrong, normal or strange, and they are primarily influenced by our upbringing and culture.

If you grew up in a culture that values collectivism, where the group's needs are placed above the individuals', you might likely be more collaborative and value harmonious relationships. Conversely, if your culture prizes individualism, you might be more independent and feel comfortable voicing your opinions, even if they contradict the group. When discussing culture, it's tempting to see it solely as traditions, language, or cuisine. But cultural values go deeper—they subtly shape our beliefs, behaviors, and interactions. They can mold our perspective toward the various dimensions of our identity, often influencing how we interpret and navigate our world.

It's important to remember our identity and cultural values are interconnected and constantly affecting each other.

This is called intersectionality, where different aspects of our identity and cultural values blend like colors on a canvas. It's what makes our experiences unique and shaped by multiple factors that shape who we are (Livermore 2009, 122).

Let's take gender as an example. A person's cultural background can significantly influence their gender identity experience. Some cultures have rigid gender roles and expectations, while others embrace more fluid expressions. So, a person identifying as nonbinary will experience their identity differently in these varying cultural contexts. In some cultures, religious beliefs are closely intertwined with daily life and form a significant part of a person's identity.

Conversely, religion might be a private matter in more secular cultures and not as strongly tied to one's identity. Then, we have socioeconomic status, often a less discussed but highly impactful dimension. Cultural values can shape our attitudes toward wealth, work ethics, and social mobility. They can affect our perceptions of poverty and wealth while influencing our aspirations and life choices.

In understanding these intersections, we must recognize the concept of intersectionality—the idea these dimensions do not exist independently but interact with each other. For instance, a person's experience as an older, low-income woman from a particular ethnic background is not just the sum of being older, low-income, a woman, and from that ethnicity. Each aspect interacts with the others, resulting in a unique lived experience.

Understanding this interaction between multiple identity dimensions and cultural values is vital as it informs our understanding of our own and others' lived experiences. Recognizing and understanding these intricacies is critical to the meaningful, respectful connections recipe. It highlights that we are all complex beings with diverse influences shaping our identities and lives. Recognizing this complexity can lead to greater empathy, more nuanced conversations, and a richer understanding of our world. After all, isn't the multitude of colors what makes a painting magnificent? Because, in the end, we are not just individuals but parts of a beautiful, intricate mosaic that is humanity.

AYESHA

Ayesha, a Pakistani Muslim woman, moved to New York City for her graduate studies in technology. Ayesha describes her religion, ethnicity, gender, age, and immigration status as the various dimensions of her identity.

But these dimensions do not exist in isolation. They interact and intersect, shaping Ayesha's experiences, beliefs, and behavior. Her cultural values, the principles and ideals she has grown up with, function like a thread that weaves through these dimensions, influencing how she and the world around her perceive and interpret them.

Being a Muslim, Ayesha observes the practices of her faith, including wearing a hijab and observing prayers five times a day. Her faith, a significant part of her identity, influences her behavior and daily routine. However, the practice of her faith is also influenced by her cultural values, shaped by her Pakistani background. For instance, how she expresses her faith, the customs she follows, and the festivals she celebrates might differ from a Muslim person from a different ethnic background.

As a woman in a largely male-dominated academic field, Ayesha often finds herself in situations where her cultural values of respect and modesty are challenged. However, her values also strengthen her, helping her navigate challenges and assert her identity.

"They are my compass," she says.

Moving to New York was a significant culture shock.

"This place is very different than my home country, and I am always confronted due to my immigration status," she explains.

Different aspects of her identity are always highlighted, from the food she eats to the clothes she wears to the language she speaks. Ayesha relies on her cultural values to navigate the different dimensions of her identity. These values help her figure out how to approach new situations and connections.

The intersections of her identity dimensions are not mere crossroads. They are vibrant, bustling intersections that give rise to unique experiences influenced by her cultural values.

Understanding how our cultural values intersect with different parts of who we are can help us appreciate how unique our experiences are. It also helps us understand and empathize with others. Like Ayesha, we all have unique intersections that guide us based on our cultural compass.

LAURA

Laura is a middle-aged African-American woman working as a managing director in a finance services consulting group. Each of these dimensions of Laura's identity—her age, gender, race, and profession—doesn't exist in a vacuum. They interact with each other and are influenced by her cultural values.

As a woman in a male-dominated field, Laura often finds herself navigating a world designed primarily for her male counterparts. Her lived experiences, opportunities, and challenges in this industry are vastly different from those of her male colleagues, shaping her professional journey in unique ways.

Her cultural values, shaped by her African-American heritage, also influence her lived experience. These values often influence her perspectives, decision-making, and interactions in the workplace.

"They give me the strength and resilience to break down barriers and carve out a space for myself in this industry," she explains.

Another layer to her identity is her age. As a middle-aged woman, Laura's experiences are very different from those of younger women in the same field. The challenges she faced as she built her career, molded by the intersectionality of her gender, age, and career, shaped her experience differently from her younger counterparts.

"They have way more options than I did at their age," she tells me.

ALEX

Alex is a white homosexual male living in a southern US city known for its conservative values. Alex comes from a traditional family background deeply rooted in religious beliefs. This intersection of his cultural and personal identities presents unique challenges and conflicts.

"I wish they understood me and accepted me for who I am. I love them unconditionally, but they don't feel the same for me," he said when I asked him about his relationship with his family.

Alex has always deeply respected his family's faith and dedication to community service, inheriting these values himself. However, the tension between the conservative values of his family and his sexual orientation has been a source of internal conflict. While Alex has come to accept his identity as a gay man, he struggles with the fear of rejection from his family and community.

At work, the situation gets more challenging. Alex is employed at a well-established law firm, an environment dominated by heterosexual men and characterized by traditional values.

The firm prizes long hours and competitiveness and is not known for its openness to diversity, clashing with Alex's inherent value of community service and cooperation.

In the workplace, Alex struggles with the reality of having to compartmentalize his life. He fears that coming out may lead to potential discrimination or hinder his career progression within the firm. This sentiment has strained his relationships with colleagues as he constantly withholds aspects of his personal life.

Alex also finds himself in an emotional tug-of-war when building trust. In his private life, he values open and genuine relationships where trust is built through emotional connection and authenticity. However, in the office, he's found that trust often hinges on professional competence and conforming to the company's traditional norms, limiting his ability to foster deep, meaningful relationships with his colleagues.

Though Alex grapples with these challenges, he also sees them as opportunities. He's joined a local LGBTQ+ professionals group where he can share his experiences and get advice from those who've navigated similar paths. He's also started advocating subtly within his firm for more inclusive practices, leveraging his legal expertise to present compelling arguments about the value of diversity in the workplace.

Alex's story underscores the complex intersections of cultural values and personal identities and the difficulties faced when these aspects clash. However, it also highlights the courage required to navigate these challenges and the opportunity for growth and change they may represent.

Each dimension—gender, race, age, profession, and more—influences and is influenced by the others. They don't just add up. They interact and intersect, like the myriads of threads in different colors and textures that weave together to form a unique tapestry of experiences. This is the crux of intersectionality.

PRIORITY

Imagine each aspect of our identity as a different instrument in a grand orchestra. Each instrument has a unique tone and melody, contributing to the harmony of the whole piece. Each carries a unique sound, a unique value. Think about the role conductors play in orchestras. They don't play an instrument themselves, but they guide the performance, bringing each instrument into focus at the right time. Our cultural values function much like this conductor. They guide how we understand and value each dimension of our identity (Livermore 2009, 122).

Growing up in a culture that highly values tradition and family ties may greatly influence your priorities. You may prioritize family gatherings, continuing family traditions, and making decisions in your family's best interests. On the other hand, if you come from a culture that emphasizes self-expression and individuality, you may prioritize your professional identity instead. Your career choices, dedication to your work, and ambition may be integral parts of your self-image.

Cultural values can influence how you view and appreciate different parts of your identity, like gender, religion, or socio-economic status. For instance, if your culture places great importance on gender equality, you may support equal rights for all individuals, regardless of gender.

Simply put, our cultural values act as a lens that shapes how we perceive and value different aspects of our identity. Recognizing this interconnection can provide insight into why we prioritize certain elements of our identity, hold specific beliefs, and behave in certain ways. This journey of self-discovery can be fascinating and help us understand ourselves and others better. This is essential to building cultural intelligence (Livermore 2009, 13).

PERSPECTIVE

Reflecting on the various facets of your identity, their influence, and how they might interplay in different life situations is crucial to understanding your and others' diverse human experiences.

Think about your identity dimensions: What are the different dimensions of your identity? These include nationality, ethnicity, gender, religion, socio-economic status, and neurodiversity. Make a list of these dimensions and rate them in the order of priority.

Reflect on their importance: How important is each dimension to you? How much value do you ascribe to each one? Does your nationality precede your profession, or is it the other way around? Remember, there's no right or wrong answer. It's about your perspective.

Consider the cultural influence: Now, consider the cultural values you grew up with or live by. How have these values influenced your importance in each dimension of your identity? For example, if your culture emphasizes family and community, do you find you value your role within your family and community more?

Imagine different scenarios: Picture different scenarios and observe how these dimensions interact with each other and your cultural values. For instance, if offered a job in a foreign country, how would your cultural values intersect with your professional ambitions and ties to your home country?

Practice empathy: Finally, try to put yourself in someone else's shoes. Choose a friend or a colleague and imagine how their identity dimensions and cultural values might intersect. This exercise can help you appreciate the diversity of experiences and perspectives around you.

Remember, this journey of self-discovery and understanding others is not a one-time process. It's an ongoing conversation with yourself and the world around you. It's about continually learning, growing, and appreciating the beautifully diverse tapestry of human experiences. So, take your time, and enjoy the journey!

CHAPTER 2

What *Emily in Paris* Learns About CQ

Culturally intelligent innovation begins with changing our impulse from 'Why can't you see it like I do?' to 'Help me see what I might be missing!'

—*DAVID LIVERMORE*

OH, EMILY!

Oh no! She did not just do that. Watching *Emily in Paris* (Fleming 2020), I noticed many parallels in my life as Emily Cooper's cultural faux pas struck a chord with me, sparking my curiosity to dig deeper. *Emily in Paris* is a Netflix show depicting the protagonist's new life in Paris (Fleming 2020). She is a marketing executive in Chicago who is asked to move and teach their new French counterparts how to do things the "American" way. Emily is excited and anticipates the experience from the lens of American naivete when she learns she is being transferred to Paris. However, the stand-offish behavior of her French colleagues quickly repels her excitement when they take offense at her American manners (Fleming 2020).

Emily's behavior resonated with my cultural experiences. It aired in October 2020, at the peak of my cultural awakening journey and magnified by the COVID-19 pandemic. The pandemic was a perfect time for an awakening. This was my opportunity to amplify my voice. During this time, I began to understand why emotional intelligence fell short in my personal and professional life and why CQ was the fuel I longed for.

Emily commits several critical blunders from the beginning. She does not know the language, yet complains to her coworkers about how strange the French language is. Yikes! She also complains about each cultural difference she encounters. On her first day, she schedules a meeting with the French team and begins to speak English without asking everyone if they speak English. On her second day, Emily arrives at the office very early only to realize her French colleagues get there an hour later and then questions them why they were not in the office earlier. Later that day, she tries to invite everyone to lunch, but they vehemently reject her invitation. Emily goes out to lunch alone and runs into her coworker Luke, who stops by to say hello to her. Luke explains to Emily that the group fears her because she lives to work and worries they must work harder. Emily apologizes for offending him and visually processes the new insight (Fleming 2020).

Like Emily, I often remember thinking, *Why is everyone spending so much time talking about their personal life when we have important work to do?* As a hyperprivate person, I always felt that talking about my personal life at work was unprofessional. I, therefore, kept pleasantries on a superficial level. I often wondered whether my hyperprivate inclinations morphed from my career in human resources, my Anglo mentality, or both. Whatever it was, it prevented me from connecting deeper with coworkers from diverse cultures for many years.

At first, I believed I understood different cultures well, but I soon realized my perspective needed to be expanded and more balanced. Then, I discovered the concept of cultural intelligence (CQ), a continuous learning process about understanding and relating with different people. Just like SQ and EQ, CQ can be developed without limits. Like a labyrinth, the cultural intelligence journey can be challenging and humbling, with many twists and turns, each leading to deeper understanding and self-discovery. While studying cultural intelligence, I embarked on a passage of self-discovery that taught me important lessons in humility. Gradually, I recognize other cultures' diverse approaches toward various aspects beyond just the business world.

SOCIAL INTELLIGENCE (SQ)

Daniel Goleman (2007, 11) defines social intelligence as "a shorthand term for being intelligent not just *about* our relationships but also *in* them." In *Emily in Paris*, Emily's social intelligence skills are crucial to her success. Here are some ways Emily demonstrates her social intelligence:

Empathy and understanding: Emily often empathizes with her colleagues and friends, trying to understand their feelings and viewpoints even when they differ from hers. This is particularly evident in her relationship with her new friend Mindy, whose career struggles are supported by Emily's empathy (Fleming 2020).

Building and maintaining relationships: Emily uses her social intelligence to develop and maintain relationships with diverse people professionally and personally. For instance, despite their initial differences, she holds a respectful relationship with her boss, Sylvie. She befriends her neighbor, Gabriel, showing her ability to foster connections (Fleming 2020).

Conflict resolution: Emily demonstrates her social intelligence skills in resolving conflicts. An example is when she successfully negotiates a compromise with Pier, who is upset about a marketing campaign. She calms him down, listens to his concerns, and finds a solution for everyone (Fleming 2020).

Navigating social situations: Emily can navigate complex social situations with finesse. For instance, she learns and adapts to French social norms despite her initial faux pas. Before attending a Parisian show, she prepares and does her homework to learn about the designers who will be attending and some French phrases. During the show, she listens more than she speaks, paying close attention to conversation cues, body language, and the general social dynamics. For instance, Emily needs help understanding Antoine's relationship dynamic with his wife, Christine, and his mistress, Silvie. Instead of bluffing her way through, she asks Mindy insightful questions, signaling her interest and willingness to learn. This adaptability reflects her ability to read and respond to social cues effectively (Fleming 2020).

Influence and persuasion: Emily often uses her social intelligence to influence others and persuade them to see her point of view. An example is when she persuades a designer to work with her firm on a new campaign despite his initial reluctance.

EMOTIONAL INTELLIGENCE (EQ)

EQ refers to the ability to self-motivate and continue pushing through challenges, exercise self-control and postpone immediate rewards, manage emotional responses so that stress doesn't inhibit clear thinking, and possess empathy and optimism (Goleman 1995, 52).

In Emily's professional life, she deals with stakeholders—her boss, colleagues, and clients—all with different personalities, work styles, and expectations. Understanding and navigating these emotional complexities is crucial for her professional success (Fleming 2020).

In her personal life, Emily's EQ also helps her build and maintain relationships with new friends and love interests in Paris. Let's consider Emily's budding friendship with Mindy, the lively au pair she meets in the park. She recognizes Mindy's outgoing nature and quickly establishes a rapport, finding common ground in their shared experience as expats in Paris. Mindy is a breath of fresh Parisian air and an invaluable support system, but their friendship doesn't happen instantly. Emily's EQ comes into play when she tunes into Mindy's emotions and experiences. For instance, when Mindy shares her story of a failed singing audition, Emily doesn't dismiss or belittle her feelings. Instead, she empathizes and encourages Mindy to chase her dreams again. This emotional sensitivity strengthens their bond and lays a solid foundation for their friendship. Understanding and responding to Mindy's emotions helps Emily build a deep bond and trust with her. Understanding her own emotions and those of others enables her to handle interpersonal relationships judiciously and empathetically.

Then there's Gabriel, the handsome French chef living below Emily's apartment, who manages to stir not just delectable dishes but also a whirlwind of emotions in Emily. Her EQ helps Emily balance her feelings and maintain a respectful relationship with Gabriel, who is already in a relationship with her friend Camille. She manages to handle this complicated love triangle without causing unnecessary harm to their friendships by being aware of her feelings and understanding and respecting the feelings of Gabriel and Camille (Fleming 2020).

And who could forget the time Emily had to deal with Mathieu, her client's nephew, with whom she shares a romantic connection? Here, too, Emily's EQ is put to the test when she must navigate the tricky waters of workplace relationships. She considers Mathieu's feelings and the implications of their relationship on her professional life. It's a delicate balance, and she manages it by understanding her emotions and those of others involved (Fleming 2020).

It is striking how Emily's experiences show how important emotional intelligence is. She adapts to new surroundings and deals with different personal and professional scenarios using her emotional intelligence in very ingenious ways (Fleming 2020).

Self-awareness: Emily is good at self-awareness, which is essential for emotional intelligence. For example, she knows she needs help understanding French culture and sometimes has trouble communicating because of the language barrier. Emily recognizes she is a foreigner in Paris and doesn't speak the language fluently. Rather than ignoring or downplaying this fact, she openly acknowledges it and uses it as motivation to learn and adapt to her new environment. She is honest with herself and others about these challenges, which shows that she can recognize her emotions and how they affect her interactions with people (Fleming 2020).

Self-regulation: Emily is good at understanding emotions and knows how to handle different situations. She is exceptionally skilled at staying positive when dealing with demanding clients or cultural differences. Emily frequently faces criticism from her boss, Sylvie, who initially is not welcoming or supportive. Despite this, Emily can regulate her emotional responses, maintaining professionalism and focusing on her work rather than retaliating or reacting impulsively (Fleming 2020).

Motivation: Emily always stays motivated. Even when things get tough and obstacles arise, she keeps her passion and dedication to her job. Emily does not let cultural differences hinder her. Her motivation to understand and appreciate French culture and the way of doing things, whether it's food, fashion, or work ethics, speaks volumes about her determination to succeed. Her willingness to adapt and unwavering resilience help her overcome anything that comes her way and reach her goals (Fleming 2020).

Empathy: Emily is good at understanding other people's feelings and opinions. She's especially great at empathizing with her French colleagues and friends, even if she does not always agree. Emily's French colleagues initially display resentment toward her, especially her boss, Sylvie. Despite the cold reception, Emily tries to understand their perspectives and the cultural differences that might contribute to their reactions. This understanding is a clear demonstration of empathy.

Social skills: Emily demonstrates stellar social skills. She communicates well and readily resolves conflicts. Despite her limited fluency in the language and customs, she's even able to navigate the social dynamic complexities with her French colleagues, friends, and romantic partners. Emily must communicate effectively with various stakeholders, including colleagues, clients, and influencers. Despite cultural and language barriers, Emily excels at expressing her ideas clearly and persuasively. She knows how to build and maintain relationships effectively. Even when there is conflict, she focuses on rebuilding the relationship.

EQ is necessary for personal and professional development. Still, other skills are required in a multicultural environment like the one Emily navigates in Paris. There are several reasons why EQ alone may not be enough for Emily:

Cultural understanding: EQ might help Emily understand and manage her emotions and those of others, but it does not necessarily provide the skills for understanding cultural nuances like the bureaucracy of terminating someone's job (Fleming 2020). Paris has a culture very different from Chicago. Understanding these cultural nuances—such as attitudes toward work-life balance, directness in communication, and social customs—requires cultural intelligence (CQ).

Behavioral adaptation: While EQ can help Emily empathize with her colleagues, it does not equip her with the skills to navigate different cultural norms that impact how empathy is expressed and perceived (Fleming 2020). This is where CQ comes in, guiding her to behave appropriately in various settings and helping her avoid cultural faux pas.

Interpreting emotions in different cultures: People from different cultures generally express emotions differently. A typical emotional response in one culture might be inappropriate and even offensive in another. Without understanding the cultural context (which CQ provides), Emily might misinterpret the emotions and reactions of those around her despite her high EQ (Fleming 2020).

Cultural miscommunication: Even if Emily can understand and manage emotions well, it does not necessarily mean she can communicate effectively in a different cultural setting (Fleming 2020). Each culture has its communication norms and styles, and understanding this is a part of CQ, not EQ. Misinterpreting these cultural communication norms can lead to significant misunderstanding, miscommunication, and conflict, even with high EQ.

Coping with culture shock: Moving to a new country with a different culture, language, and norms can be stressful and disorienting. While EQ can help manage stress and anxiety, understanding and adapting to a new culture—the essence of CQ—is crucial to deal with this culture shock effectively.

CQ, WHERE HAVE YOU BEEN ALL MY LIFE?

Emily has moved from Chicago to Paris, two cities with drastically different cultures. Her ability to adapt and function effectively in this new cultural context, essentially CQ, is critical to her success (Fleming 2020). It is a form of intelligence tested and found to be crucial in today's increasingly global and intercultural world. Learning about and understanding French cultural norms and expectations helps her adjust her behavior accordingly and communicate and interact effectively with the locals. Blending SQ, EQ, and CQ helps Emily survive and thrive in her new environment (Fleming 2020).

David Livermore highlights the combination of EQ and CQ in his book *Cultural Intelligence: Improving Your CQ to Engage Our Multicultural World*. "With emotional intelligence, we know how to act and relate to others when we're in our own cultural context. Cultural Intelligence picks up where EQ leaves off by dealing with people and circumstances in unfamiliar contexts" (2009, 46).

CQ helps Emily navigate cultural misunderstandings, build strong relationships with her French colleagues and friends, and become more effective (Fleming 2020).

Thanks to her CQ, Emily adapts and thrives in Paris. She's learning to navigate cultural misunderstandings and has built strong relationships with French colleagues and friends (Fleming 2020). Throughout the show, you can see Emily flex her CQ muscles in a few ways:

> **CQ Drive (motivational CQ):** It's impressive how Emily stays motivated and positive while adjusting to a new culture despite many mishaps. Even though she's had some challenges, she's resilient and always eager to learn and grow. That kind of determination is what makes up a crucial part of CQ Drive (Fleming 2020).

> **CQ Knowledge (cognitive CQ):** Emily is working hard to learn all about French culture, from the language to how people work and live (Fleming 2020). Even though

she makes mistakes, she's determined to learn and understand the culture around her better. She uses her acquired knowledge to improve the essence of CQ Knowledge (Fleming 2020).

CQ Strategy (metacognitive CQ): She takes the time to understand French cultural norms to unlearn and relearn ways to coexist comfortably within them. She uses her knowledge to plan for better interactions. One thing she's picked up is the importance of taking long lunch breaks and their impact on building relationships. She's also learning how to best present her ideas in a way that makes sense in a French workplace (Fleming 2020). Planning and regularly checking in is what CQ Strategy is all about.

CQ Action (behavioral CQ): It's incredible seeing how Emily adapts to French culture! She can adjust her professional behavior to fit perfectly with her colleagues and clients. She's changed her communication style, shows respect for French customs, and even incorporates aspects of the French lifestyle into her daily routine (Fleming 2020). Witnessing such dedication to fitting in professionally and personally is rewarding.

EQ allows Emily to navigate her new life's emotional and interpersonal aspects. At the same time, CQ enables her to understand and adapt to cultural differences, all while remaining incredibly humble! Together, these two forms of intelligence greatly enhance her ability to succeed in her Parisian professional and personal life. It's also important to highlight that these skills don't come naturally to Emily (or anyone, for that matter). They require conscious effort, learning, and growth (Fleming 2020).

PUTTING IT ALL TOGETHER

In *The Cultural Intelligence Difference: Master the One Skill You Can't Do Without in Today's Global Economy,* David Livermore highlights differences in social, emotional, and cultural intelligence (2011, 36). According to Livermore, cultural intelligence (CQ) refers to our ability to comprehend and connect with individuals from different cultures (2011, 12). Emotional intelligence (EQ), on the other hand, involves perceiving, understanding, and managing emotions. Lastly, social intelligence (SQ) involves interacting with others and establishing relationships. Essentially, CQ is a link between EQ and SQ, as Livermore explains. This realization was a game-changer for me. "The social skills and common sense learned through emotional intelligence don't automatically translate into successful performance when applied to other cultures," Livermore writes (2011, 36).

Livermore was gracious enough to chat about his journey toward cultural intelligence. He was also drawn toward cultural intelligence to understand how to apply a globally appropriate approach to leadership development.

"The feedback I was getting on the leadership program was that it has a very Western approach," he explains.

His colleagues' feedback propelled him to focus his academic studies on cultural differences and how they influence leadership development.

"I wanted to do academic research that would help meet my own practical needs as well as the ones my colleagues were facing," he explains.

Speaking with David about applying cultural intelligence confirms the complexity behind this journey and why a commitment to lifelong learning is critical. Cultivating basic knowledge about different cultures creates a starting point for connecting deeper when engaging with diverse people. Curiosity, humility, and empathy help you understand the person better.

"You need to have foundational knowledge in a way that helps frame a discussion with someone who is different," he explains.

Cultural intelligence facilitates understanding in ways that help you adapt while maintaining your views in diverse settings. Adapting while preserving your authenticity is important here. Adapting doesn't mean adopting.

"Cultural intelligence provides a universal language that can be applied globally and adjusted according to the context. Cultural intelligence allowed me to still go about my view of the world, but also allow other people to do that," Livermore explains.

Brilliant! This is what clicked for me. Cultural intelligence helps me understand differences in a way that allows me to coexist with others who are different while keeping my values intact.

Recognizing that successfully navigating diverse relationships involves fusing CQ, SQ, and EQ has been a significant epiphany. It's essential to comprehend and adjust to cultural differences, manage emotions in ourselves and others, and cultivate multicultural relationships. This realization has also helped me in my personal life, where I am receptive to different approaches to life while interacting with people from diverse cultural backgrounds.

Although Emily is a fictional character whose actions and decisions are not always perfect or exemplary, she is a work in progress like me!

PERSPECTIVE

Understanding the differences between Cultural Intelligence (CQ), Social Intelligence (SQ), and Emotional Intelligence (EQ) can be facilitated through reflective prompts that help you gain perspective on your experiences and interactions.

Reflect on a recent cross-cultural interaction: What cultural differences did you notice? How did these differences impact the interaction? Did you adapt your behavior based on the cultural context? This can help you gauge your CQ.

Consider a recent group dynamic: Did you notice the unspoken social rules? Were you able to read the room effectively? How did you navigate any conflicts or disagreements? Reflection on these points can shed light on your SQ.

Reflect on a recent emotional experience: How did you handle your emotions? Were you aware of the emotions of others around you? Did you manage to maintain control of your emotions or react impulsively? This can help you assess your EQ.

Think about a situation where you succeeded: How did your understanding of emotional cues (EQ), social dynamics (SQ), and cultural differences (CQ) contribute to your success? This prompt can help distinguish the unique roles of EQ, SQ, and CQ in successful interactions.

Consider a challenging interpersonal interaction: Were the challenges due to cultural differences (CQ), misreading social cues (SQ), or mishandling emotions (EQ)? Or a combination of these? Identifying the roots of these challenges can help differentiate between the roles of EQ, SQ, and CQ.

Imagine moving to a different country: What skills would you need to build relationships with the locals (CQ)? How would you navigate social situations (SQ)? How would you manage the stress and emotions of living in a new place (EQ)? This hypothetical scenario can highlight the specific roles of CQ, SQ, and EQ.

CHAPTER 3

Looking in the Mirror

———

To err is human. To forgive is divine.
—*ALEXANDER POPE*

"Can I ask you a question?" I asked my colleague one day.

"What?" he says.

"Why do you always talk over me?"

"What?" he says.

"Do you realize you always talk over me?" I affirmed.

"No, I didn't realize. I'm sorry," he says.

I remember this moment well. I was in the middle of my awareness-building journey and suddenly noticed more and more cultural disparities around me. Before this moment, I always assumed he was just rude. However, after I learned more about my cultural values and cultural intelligence, I realized my colleague comes from a region with a different perspective of time.

It was hard to admit I had some prejudices, but I knew it was essential to confront them. Although it took some time to work through my feelings, I ultimately learned from my mistakes.

A place of wonder and desire to dig deeper emerged. *What does this mean to me? How does this impact who I am? How I show up in the world? How I speak, lead, coexist?* I felt like I had just woken up from a coma, and everything seemed both exciting and overwhelming at the same time. I had to confront my biases head-on and couldn't rely on my old way of thinking. However, I gained a newfound appreciation for the lessons I was learning.

I was so excited to share my new knowledge with everyone around me! Suddenly, I sprinkled little tidbits into conversations with friends and colleagues.

"I don't think I can trust them," my colleague said about a candidate we just interviewed.

"Why not?" I asked.

"They did not look at me directly when answering my questions."

"Did you know that in some cultures, it is considered rude and confrontational to look someone directly in the eye?"

"Really?" she asked.

"Yes, and it may also be related to neurodiversity."

"Wow. I had no idea. Thank you for telling me that," she said.

What created such a shift in me? Shame about my igno-rance drove the transformation in me. However, this shame sparked my curiosity and made me more aware. I combined my curiosity with a strong sense of responsibility to edu-cate those around me and became an ally. For me, this was personal.

CONFRONTING MY BIASES

It would be great if everyone wanted to eliminate their biases, but awareness alone is not enough, especially in our increas-ingly polarized society.

When Emily first sets foot in Paris, she is brimming with anticipation (Fleming 2020). However, her optimism is soon met with a few challenging realities. As an American in Paris, Emily faces a cultural landscape much different than she is used to. There are subtle differences in the work ethic, social etiquette, and communication style, which initially frustrate her. She quickly judges her French counterparts, labeling them overly relaxed, impolite, or blunt.

The more she thinks about it, the more Emily realizes she must step out of her comfort zone and immerse herself in French culture. Instead of viewing cultural differences as negatives, she sees them as learning opportunities. She dives into French culture and even attends French lessons (Fleming 2020).

Emily's experience in Paris becomes a journey of self-discovery and growth. Confronting her biases, Emily learns to appreciate and understand the beauty of Parisian culture and make meaningful connections with those around her (Fleming 2020). It isn't easy, but it becomes an invaluable lesson in empathy, understanding, and cultural appreciation.

KIERA

Kiera is a gifted software engineer and a proud African-American woman working in a predominantly white-male tech start-up in Silicon Valley. As the only Black woman on her team, Kiera's cultural values often conflict with those of the dominant culture at her workplace. Coming from an affective culture, Kiera is used to expressing emotions openly and forming personal bonds at work. However, her colleagues from neutral cultures often misinterpret her expressiveness as unprofessional, creating biases and leading to misunderstandings.

Kiera also comes from a background where high power distance is the norm, meaning she respects authority and hierarchy. However, her start-up culture is marked by low power distance, where everyone is encouraged to challenge ideas openly, leading to further biases about Kiera's ability to voice her thoughts and opinions. Moreover, Kiera values collectivism deeply, often focusing on group successes rather than individual achievements. However, in her individualistic work environment, Kiera's preference for teamwork sometimes makes colleagues perceive her as less ambitious or less competitive.

Kiera is committed to navigating the challenges successfully. She confronted these biases by turning to her cultural intelligence (CQ) to bridge the cultural gap. She realizes that while she can't control others' biases, she can influence their understanding and perceptions of her through thoughtful actions.

"I felt I had to do something," she explained. "I was like a fish out of water and initially felt so uncomfortable. But once I intentionally sought to educate others, I became more motivated to continue. I felt powerless and powerful at the same time. People didn't always respond, but I knew they were listening," she told me. "Little by little, people's attitude toward me shifted from adversarial to collegial."

Kiera engages in open conversations about her cultural values with her team to address misunderstandings stemming from her expressive communication style. She explains that in her culture, people express their feelings openly and that it's a sign of passion and engagement rather than unprofessionalism. Her team is not always receptive to what she has to say. Still, she relentlessly educates others while accepting them as they are.

To navigate the power distance difference, Kiera consciously steps outside her comfort zone to voice her ideas more assertively, in line with the start-up's open dialogue culture. At the same time, she also tries to highlight the value of respecting others' ideas and creating a safe space for everyone to speak.

Regarding collectivism, Kiera begins acknowledging her contributions while advocating for a more balanced perspective on teamwork in her individualistic work environment. She emphasizes how collaboration can lead to more creative solutions and innovation.

Through her high CQ, Kiera successfully navigates cultural challenges and biases. She contributes positively to her team's dynamics and productivity. She raises awareness about cultural values and the need for inclusivity in the workplace. Her story is a testament to the power of cultural intelligence in overcoming biases and promoting mutual understanding in a diverse environment.

BECOMING COMFORTABLE WITH THE UNCOMFORTABLE

Like Emily and Kiera, I was uncomfortable the first time I confronted my biases, as I saw myself in a new light. I always considered myself open-minded and fair to everyone, but then I noticed I tend to gravitate toward people who think like me. After some self-reflection, I realized I unconsciously favor similar people despite my belief in the importance of diverse perspectives.

Recognizing my bias was only the first step toward improvement. To make progress, I had to challenge my preconceptions and consciously choose to quiet them. Cultural intelligence invokes the drive to see past our biases and accept other norms and customs. It's encouraging to know we can work on improving our drive. The best way to do this is to confront our biases head-on.

I realized my go-getter attitude was the driving force behind my ambitious nature, which helped me ascend the corporate ladder. Being assertive and outspoken, I've always strived to achieve my goals. Others also shared this mindset, which helped me develop my leadership and team-building skills. However, I admit I unintentionally favored those who shared my "achievement" preferences and sometimes overlooked opinions from those with different perspectives.

We all have biases, and it's important to acknowledge them. I don't believe biases are good or bad. It's what we decide to do with them that becomes helpful or hurtful. Accepting our biases is the first step to bringing about positive change in ourselves and the world around us. Without acceptance, we can't move forward.

MINDSET

Unbiased action is your superpower. When encountering someone from a different culture, taking five seconds to see them for who they are rather than through a flawed interpretation of what they are will impact how you connect.

This experience taught me my greatest lesson: Some biases no longer serve me, while others require consistent self-management to prevent them from triggering me. For instance, my monochronic sense of time orientation led to erroneous perspectives about how people view time. Monochronic cultures, such as those in North America and Germany, tend to focus on one thing at a time and view time sequentially, while polychronic cultures, like those in France or Italy, focus on many things at once and view time in synchronic ways (Trompenaars and Woolliams 2003, 605).

As someone who follows a monochronic approach, I view time as a linear and sequential resource that influences my work. For me, deadlines mean beginning with the most crucial tasks and adhering to fixed target dates. However, this is not globally the case (Troompenaars and Woolliams 2003, 605). This is a significant bias of mine, as I used to believe time was perceived in the same way everywhere and expected others to think the same. In the past, I used to get frustrated when meetings didn't start on time, but I now understand why I got annoyed and how this annoyance distanced me from my colleagues.

Sometimes, I find myself falling back into old patterns, and while I still struggle with this bias today, grasping my time preference and how that differs from other cultures opened the door to a deeper understanding. Like Emily, I noticed a shift in my behavior as time passed. As I gained cultural awareness, my knowledge grew and my relationships deepened. I am sure some of my colleagues wondered why I never answer the phone during meetings, the same way I wonder why they insist on calling me while my "in a meeting" status is on. Each stumble is a wake-up call and reminder that the journey toward cultural intelligence is not a destination. This perspective has facilitated my work with colleagues from around the world. Using motivational interviewing techniques for self-reflection helped me deepen my understanding of cultural biases.

Robin Sharma states, "Awareness precedes choice, and choice precedes results" (2011, 141). We all have biases, and it's essential to acknowledge them to work toward positive change. According to humanistic psychologist Carl Rogers, we need a safe and accepting environment to grow and be our true selves (1959, 206). This means sharing our thoughts and feelings without fear of judgment. We can make significant changes when we accept all parts of ourselves with kindness, even our biases.

It takes a lot of courage, empathy, and openness to learn and grow to acknowledge and correct our biases. Sometimes, these biases can be sneaky and affect our actions and choices without realizing it. But it's essential to confront them head-on to make fair and informed decisions.

One helpful approach to overcoming biases is to look under the hood. Acknowledging, writing down, and deconstructing your biases helps you understand, befriend, and confront them head-on. Come along with me to the next chapter as we demystify the different cultural values and how they shape different areas of our lives.

PERSPECTIVE

Confronting biases is essential for personal growth, empathy, and effective communication. Here are a few reflective prompts to help you gain perspective about your biases and work toward overcoming them:

Identify any biases: Reflect on a situation where your initial judgment about a person or scenario was proven wrong. What assumptions did you make and why?

Consider your biases' origins: Consider your upbringing, experiences, and influences. How might they have influenced your biases?

Recognize the impact of biases: Can you recall a time when your bias may have negatively affected your interaction with someone else? How did it impact your relationship with that person?

Imagine being on the receiving end: How would you feel if someone was biased against you? How might it affect your relationship with them?

Devise strategies to overcome biases: What steps could you take to confront your biases? How could you replace snap judgments with more thoughtful, fair assessments?

Explore unfamiliar cultures or groups: Are there certain cultures, groups, or individuals you know little about and may have unconscious biases toward? How could you learn more about them to dispel stereotypes and broaden your understanding?

Challenge your own beliefs: Think about a strongly held belief. What evidence supports it? Have you considered contradictory evidence? What might it mean for you if you were wrong about this belief?

Seek diverse perspectives: How can you expose yourself to people, experiences, or media that offer viewpoints different from yours?

PART 2

WHAT HERE IS

CHAPTER 4

Cultural Values Demystified

A nation's culture resides in the hearts and in the soul of its people.
—MAHATMA GANDHI

"You must reach books that enrich your mind, not random material," my father told me.

"Yes, Papi," I said.

"Remember, you are a wife and mother now. Your wardrobe and lifestyle must reflect that," he said.

"Yes, Papi," I said.

"I brought you some vitamins that you need to take daily."

"Si, Papi."

"Did you take your vitamins today?"

"Si, Papi."

No matter how old I am, I will always follow my parent's orders. To this day, my father still tells me to be careful running because of my asthma, even though I haven't had an asthmatic episode in over twenty years!

"Don't eat junk because it steals your brain power, and I don't like it," he'll tell me.

"Yes, Papi." I comply.

I am almost fifty, and I still obey his orders. For the longest time, I thought the "children are seen, not heard" parenting perspective was a "Dominican or Latin" thing. But, learning about cultural values taught me this concept is an example of the norms in high power-distance cultures like the Dominican Republic, where respect for authority and your elders is a priority.

Becoming culturally aware starts with exploring your cultural values (Livermore 2009, 13). You know that feeling when you try a dish from a different cuisine for the first time, and you're left scrunching your face in surprise or savoring the explosion of flavors with delight? It feels like stepping outside your cultural comfort zone and immersing yourself in the global cultural buffet.

But before we hop from one cultural dish to another, let's pause for a moment and take a closer look at our own dish.

It's packed with personal cultural values, but do we really know what's in there? Let's dive in.

Our cultural values are like the seasoning to our life's dish— they spice up our behaviors, influence our decisions, and mold our perceptions. It's the familial recipes passed down, the societal norms we grow up with, and our national pride. These values shape our worldview like a pair of tinted glasses through which we see everything.

Often, we're so accustomed to wearing our glasses that we don't even realize they're there. We take them for granted, like background music that's always playing. But to truly understand and appreciate other cultures, we must first acknowledge the lens through which we view them.

So, how do we start this self-exploration journey? Think about your reactions to different situations. Are you more comfortable in a group or prefer flying solo? When facing a problem, do you tackle it head-on or consult with others first? Your responses reflect your cultural values. If you like group settings and collective decision-making, you might lean toward collectivist values. On the other hand, if autonomy and individual decision-making appeal more to you, individualistic values might resonate more with you.

Now, let's excavate a little deeper. I'd like you to reflect on your beliefs about communication, power dynamics, conflict resolution, or even something as mundane as time management. Do you prefer to communicate explicitly, or do you like to leave a message that is subject to interpretation? Do you prefer hierarchical structures or flat organizations? Do you address conflicts directly or value harmony more? Do you view time linearly, or is flexibility more your style? Your perspectives on these aspects can shed light on your power-distance orientation, approach to uncertainty, and perception of time—all critical components of your cultural values.

Understanding your cultural values is not about boxing yourself into stereotypes (Livermore 2011, 102). It's about becoming aware of your inherent preferences, which can sometimes unconsciously influence your behaviors and judgments. This self-awareness is the starting point for developing cultural competence. After all, recognizing our cultural lens allows us to understand that others might view the world through a different set.

CULTURAL VALUE DIMENSIONS

In *The Cultural Intelligence Difference: Master the One Skill You Can't Do Without in Today's Global Economy,* Livermore discusses why it's essential to understand our cultural values. "As we learn more about cultures and the different ways of doing things, it helps us better understand what's going on, which in turn helps us relate and work more effectively," Livermore writes (2011, 86).

These dimensions can benefit anyone looking to improve their cultural intelligence and understanding. They support the CQ Knowledge and CQ Strategy capabilities and form the foundation of becoming culturally intelligent.

Understanding my cultural preferences and how they influence my actions personally and professionally facilitated navigating tricky intercultural interactions at home and work. It's also helped me understand how my preferences impact my communication style, relationships, social life, and other areas.

A BIT ABOUT CULTURAL VALUES

INDIVIDUALISM-COLLECTIVISM

My first encounter with the individualism-collectivism dimension was during my first job as a director of human resources for an international conglomerate. It was tough to adjust to the collectivist culture that permeated the company culture, as I was raised in a society that valued personal autonomy and individualism. However, as time passed, I realized the importance of the collective and found ways to contribute to the group's success while respecting the need for harmony and authority. This experience helped me broaden my perspective on individualism and collectivism, and I learned to balance personal and group needs better.

POWER DISTANCE

When I first visited Mexico, I immediately grasped the significance of power distance in their culture. High power distance highlights the importance of hierarchy and respect for authority, which was an adjustment for me, coming from a culture with low power distance. I recall when I questioned the opinion of a senior executive, only to see him grimace and be uncomfortable. In Mexico, it's customary to acknowledge the views of someone with a higher ranking unless asked explicitly for your thoughts. Even when asked, one cannot be as open as they might be in American culture. This experience helped me understand how crucial it is to comprehend and respect the power dynamics unique to each culture and adjust my behavior accordingly.

UNCERTAINTY AVOIDANCE

While working on a project with some Latin American colleagues, I noticed they prefer avoiding uncertainty. In contrast, my cultural values are more comfortable with ambiguity and uncertainty. At first, I found it frustrating when they used a fixed approach to decision-making and problem-solving. However, combining our approaches cleared the roadblocks needed to craft various solutions and ideas.

TIME ORIENTATION

Time orientation refers to how much you prioritize immediate outcomes compared to results that might take years to achieve. I focus on meeting goals and targets, completing projects on time, and emphasizing quick wins and immediate gratification. In working with cultures prioritizing long-term gains, I learned that they invest time in building client relationships, focus on team development, and are willing to undertake projects that may not show immediate profits but promise significant returns in the long run. Although our time orientation differences could lead to clashes, they could complement each other if managed well. My drive for immediate results helps keep teams on track for short-term goals while blending with a long-term perspective to ensure sustainability and future success.

COOPERATIVE/COMPETITIVE

As a high achiever, I focused more on my success than on working together toward a common goal with others who value cooperation. This sometimes caused disagreements with those prioritizing mutual benefit, teamwork, and getting along. However, I've understood that collaboration can build trust, improve communication, and create lasting relationships, while competition can drive innovation, increase efficiency, and help us grow personally. Finding a balance between these values has helped me achieve better personal, professional, and organizational results without sabotaging relationships.

CONTEXT (DIRECT/INDIRECT)

During my early years as a leader in a global multinational, I gained valuable insight into cultural differences in language usage. I discovered that some cultures rely heavily on nonverbal cues and implicit understanding, while others prefer direct and explicit language. Misunderstandings can occur when individuals from different cultural backgrounds misinterpret each other's communication styles, leading to conflicts. Understanding the differences helped me better navigate goals and objectives.

BEING/DOING

I am a doer and always have been. I've realized my cultural preferences affect how I approach life. People who prioritize "being" enjoy being in the moment rather than always being busy with something. They emphasize building good relationships, staying in tune with nature, and keeping their emotional and spiritual well-being in check. To them, time is more of a cycle than a straight line, and they don't measure success just by what's been accomplished or what they own. They focus more on enjoying the process of getting there rather than achieving goals. People who prioritize "doing" tend to focus more on getting things done, being productive, accomplishing, and achieving goals. They are often goal-oriented, setting their sights on concrete objectives and working actively toward achieving them. Time is seen as a precious commodity in these cultures, and there's usually a strong emphasis on efficiency and productivity. Both approaches have pros and cons, but balancing is critical to achieving personal growth, well-being, and sustainable success. This balanced approach helps me understand and appreciate my husband of thirty years, who is heavily into "being."

UNIVERSALISM/PARTICULARISM

I'm still figuring out if my career in human resources has influenced or been influenced by my cultural values. Still, I've always believed the same rules apply to all unless circumstances require otherwise. The universalism/particularism value dimension refers to different approaches to rules, principles, and moral frameworks in social interactions. Universalism emphasizes the importance of applying fair and objective regulations and standards to everyone, regardless of context or relationship. This promotes equality, fairness, and adherence to common laws and ethical principles.

On the other hand, particularism values flexibility and adaptation, recognizing that unique responses or exceptions may be necessary in certain situations and relationships. This perspective prioritizes individual circumstances, cultural contexts, and personal relationships. Balancing universalism and particularism is essential for making effective decisions, behaving ethically, and maintaining harmonious social interactions across diverse cultural backgrounds. Rules are great, but there are times when exceptions need to be made... *maybe*?

EXPRESSIVENESS (NEUTRAL/AFFECTIVE)

I am neutral regarding expression and don't believe in the over-exertion of excitement. When I met my husband's family, on the other hand, I felt like they were either upset or arguing when they spoke. When I learned about neutral versus affective expression, I realized they were affective communicators. On one end of the spectrum, we have "affective" cultures where people freely express their feelings and emotions verbally and nonverbally. Direct eye contact, physical touch, loud voices, and animated facial expressions are often seen in these cultures, and emotional engagement is valued in relationships.

Conversely, we have "neutral" cultures where emotions are controlled and subdued, and people tend to maintain a more stoic and composed demeanor. Emotional displays are often seen as unprofessional or inappropriate, and communication is more reserved and subtle. Recognizing and appreciating cultural differences ensures effective communication across different communities. It's all about balancing verbal and nonverbal cues to help build strong relationships in various social situations. I've learned to appreciate my husband's family's affective nature to the point that I worry when they're neutral.

FOCUS (POLYCHRONIC/MONOCHRONIC)

The focus cultural value dimension is commonly used to explore how different societies manage attention and resources. In the "polychronic" end of the spectrum, cultures tend to deal with multiple tasks or issues at the same time. These societies often have a more flexible approach to schedules and deadlines, emphasizing relationships and holistic context rather than individual tasks.

On the other hand, "monochronic" cultures tend to concentrate on one task or issue at a time, favoring a linear, compartmentalized approach to work and life. These societies often prioritize punctuality, efficiency, and clear objectives. Understanding this dimension can be crucial when navigating cross-cultural interactions in personal and professional settings, as it significantly influences the approach to communication, planning, and decision-making. I'm half polychronic and half monochronic, which tremendously helps as I write this book!

EMILY

Exploring our cultural values provides insight into our behaviors and attitudes and helps us better understand those around us. They influence every aspect of our lives, subtly shaping our decisions, actions, and interactions. The patterns we trace in our daily routines and choices often stem from these deeply ingrained values.

Emily in Paris, while full of cliches, is a series that vividly illustrates how cultural value preferences impact various aspects of our lives. Emily's journey is a testament to the idea that while our preferences might be rooted in our cultural backgrounds, they are not rigid. We can adapt, learn, and grow as we encounter different cultures, shaping and enriching our experiences along the way (Fleming 2020).

Imagine waking up to a new day. Emily starts her day embodying a preference for doing, ready to seize the day and tackle her ambitious to-do list. This stems from her American cultural background, where achievement and productivity are often valued. However, she soon finds the Parisian lifestyle leans more toward being, emphasizing enjoyment in the present moment, whether eating breakfast at a café or appreciating the city's beauty and its leisure (Fleming 2020).

Her professional life in Paris vividly displays the contrast between societies. Emily, who is used to a well-structured work environment with clear expectations, grapples with the ambiguity and fluidity of her Parisian office, where adaptability is vital. Her colleagues' casual tardiness and the company's flexible deadlines initially frustrate her, but she learns to navigate this flexibility over time and even appreciates it (Fleming 2020).

Emily's preference for low-context communication initially leads to misunderstandings with her French counterparts, who value high context and subtlety. She speaks directly and explicitly when discussing business with Antoine at a party where business is not typically discussed. Emily's straightforwardness is sometimes perceived as blunt and disrespectful. Still, as she adapts, she becomes more adept at reading between the lines and respecting the unspoken rules of her new environment (Fleming 2020).

In the realm of individualism versus collectivism, Emily's American preference for individual achievements and independence comes to the forefront. She is eager to proceed with her goals to build social media for Savoir from day one, not realizing her colleagues want to know more about her before diving into social media. Yet, she learned to value the collective, understanding the importance of group harmony and consensus, especially in her professional life in Paris (Fleming 2020).

So, as we navigate through our day, our cultural values are like an invisible hand guiding our preferences, decisions, and behaviors. We're all part of this global cultural buffet, and our cultural values add unique flavors to the mix. By understanding our own, we appreciate our uniqueness and open ourselves up to the richness of others. And that makes the buffet a lot more delicious.

So, grab your fork of curiosity and plate of self-awareness, and let's start this delectable journey of cultural exploration. The buffet we will explore represents the diverse recipes that shape our preferred flavors the most. The savory dishes introduced here are balanced on communication, time orientation, power distance, conflict, and trust ingredients. Ready to awaken your senses? Bon appétit!

PERSPECTIVE

Cultural values shape our perspectives and behaviors, influencing how we interact with the world. Reflecting on these can promote a deeper self-understanding and appreciation for diversity. Use the following prompts to help you understand your cultural preferences and how they influence your behaviors and relationships.

Individualism/Collectivism: Do you prioritize personal goals or the interests of your group/community? How does this impact your decision-making process and your relationships?

Power Distance: How comfortable are you with hierarchy and power differences in your personal and professional relationships? How does this affect your interactions with supervisors, colleagues, or friends?

Uncertainty Avoidance: How do you typically react to uncertain or unpredictable situations? Do you prefer clear rules and procedures, or are you comfortable with ambiguity and spontaneity?

Cooperative/Competitive: Do you focus more on personal achievements or collective goals? How does this influence your approach to work or group tasks?

Time Orientation (Short-Term/Long-Term): Do you focus more on immediate results or long-term goals? How does this shape your life goals? How does this impact your planning and decision-making?

Context (Direct/Indirect): Do you rely more on explicit verbal information or implicit nonverbal cues? How does this influence your communication style?

Being/Doing: Do you prioritize tasks and achievements or relationships and experiences? How does this affect your work-life balance?

Universalism/Particularism: When making decisions, do you primarily rely on general rules and principles, or do you consider the specific context and the people involved? When facing an ethical dilemma, do you tend to stick to universal principles or consider unique circumstances and relationships?

Expressiveness (Neutral/Affective): How openly do you express your emotions? How does this influence your communication and interpersonal relationships?

Focus (Monochronic/Polychronic): Do you tend to focus on one task at a time until it's completed, or do you frequently switch between different tasks? When managing resources, do you prefer to invest heavily in a single project or initiative or spread your resources across multiple projects?

CHAPTER 5

A World Beyond Words

The single biggest problem in communication is the illusion it has taken place.
— *GEORGE BERNARD SHAW*

"Que?"

How can this be? I thought.

I couldn't understand what they were saying. I remember the first time I went to the Dominican Republic as an adult. My heritage is Dominican, and although I spoke Spanish fluently, I couldn't understand a word.

Wow, let me tell you, getting the hang of Dominican Spanish is like learning to dance bachata with two left feet. And the grammar rules? They're a whole other level. Phrases that might sound off in textbook Spanish, like "yo no voy no," are the norm (Bullock and Toribio 2009, 49). Plus, many old-school verb forms and word endings throw off even the most educated Dominicans. To top it off, depending on whether you're in the city or rural areas like El Cibao, the rules can change again! Trust me, it's like a rollercoaster ride for your tongue and brain (Bullock and Toribio 2009, 49).

EMILY

Emily's move to Paris is a dream come true, but she soon realizes the "City of Light" is not just about croissants and Eiffel Tower selfies. The real challenges begin when she tries to navigate the maze of French communication in her professional life and new social circle (Fleming 2020). Here's how her journey unfolds in a relatable way:

Work is her first battleground. Emily enters her Parisian office with high school French and a pocket translator, only to discover her colleagues are masters of subtlety. A casual "How are you?" can be a polite inquiry or a loaded question. She makes embarrassing mistakes, like calling her boss by his first name or missing the ironic humor in a coworker's comment (Fleming 2020).

Then there are the daily life nuances. She tries to communicate with the building manager about securing a plumber, and her message gets lost in translation. And let's not even talk about when she accidentally offends a server by ordering the wrong thing.

Emily's social life isn't smooth sailing either. Making friends is trickier than she thinks. The casual American approach to friendship doesn't quite translate in Paris. She learns that double kissing a new acquaintance on the cheeks might be considered too forward, while failing to do so in another setting might be considered cold.

But Emily is nothing if not determined. She starts taking French lessons, immerses herself in French films, and practices with friendly neighbors. She embraces those awkward moments as learning opportunities rather than embarrassing failures (Fleming 2020).

Over time, she finds herself adapting. She understands the unwritten communication rules, like the delicate art of conversation and the importance of timing, tone, and body language. She starts to appreciate the beauty of nuance and the richness of communicating with a deeper understanding of cultural context.

Slowly but surely, Emily becomes a part of the tapestry of Parisian life. She makes friends, succeeds in her job, and even manages to charm the waiter she accidentally offends.

Emily's adventure in Paris is a testament to the fact that communication is never just about the words we say. It's about understanding, empathy, patience, and the willingness to step out of our comfort zone. Her story is a relatable reminder that the road to belonging in a new place is sometimes paved with missteps, misunderstandings, and lots of learning.

And guess what? That's perfectly okay. Because at the end of the day, those awkward moments, those blunders, and those lessons learned make her experience in Paris unique and unforgettable. Emily's Parisian chapter is not just about the beautiful sights and sounds but about growth, resilience, and the joy of connecting with a new culture on a profoundly personal level.

Emily's story is an inspiring tale of adaptability, growth, and the joy of embracing a new culture. Her journey reminds us that communication is not merely about words but encompasses various cultural expressions, social norms, and personal connections. By approaching her new life with an open mind and a willingness to learn, Emily immerses herself in Paris's enchanting world and enriches her life in ways she never anticipated. Her experience in Paris becomes not just a chapter in her life but a cherished part of her personal growth and self-discovery (Fleming 2020).

LOST IN TRANSLATION

Oh, the joys of communication! We talk, we laugh, we connect. But when cultural differences enter the picture, what seems like a straightforward conversation can suddenly feel like trying to solve a Rubik's Cube blindfolded.

Ever find yourself lost in translation—even when everyone's speaking English? Welcome to the subtle, fascinating world of cultural context. It's not just about the words we say. It's about the unwritten rules that govern how we say them.

Edward Hall, a groundbreaking American anthropologist, gives us a lens to understand this phenomenon. He identifies time, space, and context as the three critical cultural differences that impact communication, dividing them into low and high-context categories. It's a framework that explains why we can be fluent in a language like Spanish and still feel utterly disoriented (Hall 1973, 177, 178). According to Hall, when people with different cultural backgrounds communicate, they bring their assumptions and expectations. These "silent languages" include nonverbal cues, social norms, and deep-seated values that shape our interactions (Hall 1977, 81–84). Communication is largely based on cultural understandings that are often unspoken within a particular cultural group, which unfortunately can sometimes lead to miscommunication, causing something to be "lost in translation" (Hall, 1977, 81–84).

I can certainly relate. I must ask my husband to translate half the time I visit the Dominican Republic. The language is Spanish, but the words sound entirely foreign to me. Every place has its way of speaking, and the Dominican Republic is no different. They speak Spanish but with a twist! They may have their accent, words, and colloquial verbiage that make their Spanish unique.

Or imagine you're British, landing in the United States. You expect smooth communication since you speak the same language. But then something odd happens. You find yourself endlessly explaining yet feeling misunderstood.

"Where can I get some trainers?" you ask your American friend in Atlanta. But then you get confused when they take you to their favorite shoe store with no sneakers!

Is it culture shock? And if it is, how can it strike so close to home?

It's an intriguing question, isn't it? The answer lies in recognizing that culture isn't just about language. It's about the nuanced dance of communication beyond words. Whether it's Asia, Europe, or the Americas, each culture has its rhythm, rules, and understanding of time, space, and context. And those unseen forces can trip us up, leaving us frustrated and puzzled, even when the words are all too familiar.

This is more than an academic curiosity. It's a practical challenge for anyone working, traveling, or engaging across cultures. It's a reminder that genuine understanding requires more than fluency. It demands empathy, curiosity, and a willingness to see the world through others' eyes. And isn't that what communication is all about?

Cross-cultural communication isn't just about talking to people from other countries. It's about understanding the invisible thread that connects us all: culture. And guess what? Culture doesn't stop at national borders.

Culture shapes our words, gestures, and pauses between our sentences, whether in a bustling Tokyo street or a quiet Midwest town. It's a complex dance that can turn a casual chat into many misunderstandings, especially when language barriers enter the scene.

But why should we care about cross-cultural communication? It's not just a nice skill to have. It's a bridge to a more connected world. When we take the time to understand what drives others, we're not just avoiding conflict but opening the door to richer relationships and deeper insights into what makes us all human.

Culture is like an iceberg: The tip may be what you see, but what's beneath the surface can trip you up. Language, of course, is a significant barrier. But what about the subtler differences, those invisible factors influenced by culture that can turn a simple conversation into a riddle?

We might stumble across unexpected cultural divides even within our "own" culture. Have you ever felt a bit lost when talking to someone from a different generation or social background? That's culture at play again, making us realize we're all part of various cultural spheres that overlap and intersect in fascinating ways.

And here's a twist: What if the culture shock comes not from speaking with someone from a different continent but from someone within your own culture—or at least, what you thought was your own culture? It's like suddenly discovering your familiar dance partner has entirely new moves.

This isn't just an intellectual exercise. It's a daily reality for many of us in our interconnected world. It's an invitation to approach each interaction with curiosity, empathy, and a readiness to learn. It's a reminder that communicating across cultures isn't about finding a common language. It's about discovering a shared humanity.

Picture yourself at a busy marketplace in Tokyo. The vendor understands your unspoken request with a glance and a subtle nod. A half world away, a businessperson insists on spelling out every deal detail in a New York City conference room. Two different scenes, two different ways of communicating, both shaped by the invisible hand of culture.

The message isn't always in the words in high-context cultures, often found in Asia, Africa, and Latin America. It's in the silence between the words, the gestures, the tone, and even the history shared by the people in the conversation. It's like reading a novel where the most essential information isn't on the page but hidden in the subtext.

If you come from a low-context culture, like those prevailing in North America and Western Europe, this can feel like trying to solve a puzzle with half the pieces missing. People in low-context cultures tend to be clear and explicit. They aim to leave no room for doubt, spelling out their intentions in no uncertain terms.

But it gets intriguing here: What happens when these two worlds converge? Imagine a Latin American executive, seasoned in indirect communication, sitting across the negotiating table from a German counterpart who expects directness. Sparks can fly, confusion may reign, and both parties may leave the table feeling misunderstood.

Why? While the Latin American executive might perceive the German's straightforwardness as brash, the German might find the Latin American's subtleness evasive. It's not just a language barrier. It's a clash of communication styles rooted in cultural norms.

In many high-context cultures, you may be expected to read the room, sense the unspoken emotions, and navigate the conversation like a boat through a winding river. In low-context cultures, it's more like driving on a straight highway: The signs are clear, and the path is marked.

These differences aren't just intriguing. They're essential to understanding our interconnected world. Whether you're closing a business deal or making a friend, recognizing whether you're in a high-context or low-context situation can be the key to successful communication.

THE ICEBERG

Figure 1 Unsplash: Simon Lee

Imagine you're at a business meeting in a foreign country, and the room is filled with tension, though you can't quite put your finger on it. Or picture yourself in an energetic street market halfway across the world, sensing intriguing connections and traditions just beyond your grasp. What's happening in these scenarios? You're bumping into the unseen 90 percent of an iceberg—the part of culture beneath the surface, invisible but powerful.

Culture is like an iceberg, a concept brilliantly depicted by Edward T. Hall (1977, 57). Above the waterline, you have the 10 percent that's visible: the language, the food, the way people dress, the public celebrations. This is the "what" of culture. It's fascinating, colorful, and often charming, but it's only the tip of the iceberg.

Dive beneath the surface, and you'll discover the remaining 90 percent, the "why" of culture. This is where things get complex and genuinely captivating. This hidden part of culture is divided into two levels: the shallow and the deep.

In the shallow part, you'll find unspoken rules that stir emotions, such as courtesy, personal space, and notions of beauty, leadership, or cleanliness. Have you ever felt uneasy when someone stands too close to you? Or wondered why a particular gesture is considered polite in one place and rude in another? You're navigating the shallow culture.

Go deeper, and you'll find the unconscious rules that can trigger intense emotional reactions. These things shape our understanding of the world, such as group decision-making, the idea of the "self," and attitudes toward competition, cooperation, and even insanity. You might never know these cultural nuances unless you plunge into the deep end.

Why does this matter? Because every interaction you have with someone from a different culture is a dance with this iceberg. The 90 percent that's hidden influences nonverbal communication, such as beliefs, attitudes, values, and emotions. It's what can turn a simple conversation into a minefield of misunderstandings and emotional reactions.

And here's the real twist: You only know these hidden rules exist once you encounter someone who doesn't play by them. It's like learning a new game while playing it because the rules are never fully explained.

In a world where understanding and empathy are more valuable than ever, taking the time to appreciate both the seen and unseen aspects of culture is not just enlightening—it's essential.

SARAH

Sarah is an accomplished marketing manager from Seattle who recently transferred to her company's branch in Baton Rouge, Louisiana. While both cities are within the United States, the cultural nuances, especially regarding communication values, are distinct. Raised in a diverse and progressive community, Sarah's values are rooted in openness, inclusivity, and direct communication. Her multicultural background shaped her understanding of different cultures, and her education honed her critical thinking and empathy skills.

Her multifaceted identity includes her West Coast upbringing, gender, educational background, and professional field. Her progressive ideals and direct communication style are significant aspects of her professional persona.

After relocating to Baton Rouge, Sarah encounters a new set of cultural norms impacting her communication style, social dynamics, workplace expectations, and relationships. Her colleagues in Louisiana value polite, indirect communication and close personal relationships, contrasting with her more direct, task-oriented style. The workplace culture in Baton Rouge emphasizes tradition and community ties, sometimes at odds with Sarah's progressive values. Teamwork, leadership, and conflict resolution expectations differ, leading to misunderstandings and friction.

"I did not know what cultural intelligence was, but I knew I wanted to create a sense of community," she told me.

Sarah takes time to observe her new colleagues' interactions, reflecting on the differences and similarities to her communication style. She initiates open and respectful conversations with her team to understand their preferences and explain her communication approach, fostering mutual understanding. She consciously adjusts her communication style to align more closely with her colleagues' expectations, balancing directness with tact and empathy. She invests in building personal relationships with her colleagues, attending social gatherings, and participating in community events to understand their values and traditions. Sarah seeks feedback and continues to learn from her experiences, embracing a growth mindset and being flexible to change.

"Little by little, I learn to manage my communication style to help the team understand me better," she explains. "I even learned some colloquial terms like 'pass a good time,' which means to have a good time." She admitted, "I didn't realize making small changes to how I communicated helped the team communicate more with me."

Sarah's ability to recognize and adapt to the cultural differences in communication values within her new workplace in Louisiana, guided by her cultural intelligence, allows her to build strong relationships with her colleagues and thrive in her new role.

Her success does not come from abandoning her values but from recognizing that different cultural contexts require nuanced approaches. She bridges the cultural gap by engaging with her colleagues, reflecting on her practices, and making practical adjustments.

This scenario underlines the importance of cultural intelligence, not just in international settings but also within the diverse cultural landscapes of a country like the United States. Sarah's story illustrates how practical CQ strategies can successfully navigate cultural challenges, promoting understanding, collaboration, and growth locally and globally.

Investing in understanding and adapting to different cultural communication norms is more than a skill. It's necessary today. We enrich our personal and professional lives by building bridges, fostering collaboration, and creating a more empathetic and inclusive environment. Embracing cultural diversity in communication is like learning a new dance. It might initially feel awkward, but you find the rhythm with practice, patience, and a willingness to learn.

So, remember the iceberg next time you're engaged in cross-cultural communication. Be aware that for every visible practice or tradition, there's a hidden world of unspoken rules and deeply ingrained beliefs. Acknowledging and exploring this hidden dimension helps build bridges, cultivate connections, and navigate human culture's rich, intricate tapestry.

PERSPECTIVE

Reflecting on our communication preferences may help us better understand our communication cultural preferences. It also helps recognize potential growth or adaptation areas when interacting with diverse groups or individuals.

Communication style: How do I usually communicate with others? Am I more direct or indirect? Do I prefer formal or informal communication? Why? How does my cultural background influence the way I express myself?

Nonverbal cues: How much do I rely on tone of voice, facial expressions, and body language in understanding others? Do I expect others to read my nonverbal cues? How do I feel when they don't?

Context understanding: How important is understanding the context (e.g., the relationship between the speakers and the situation) in my communication? Do I prefer high-context (more implicit and nuanced) or low-context (clear and direct) communication?

Relationship building: How does my communication style change with strangers versus close friends or family? Do I value building deep connections before discussing significant matters?

Conflict resolution: How do I handle disagreements or conflicts in communication? How does my cultural background influence my approach to conflict?

Technology and communication: How comfortable am I with using technology (emails, texts, video calls) for communication? Do I feel technology enhances or hinders my authentic communication?

Group dynamics: How do I communicate in group settings? Do I speak up, or do I prefer to listen? How do my cultural norms influence my behavior in group communications?

Adaptability: How adaptable am I in my communication style when interacting with people from different cultures? Have I ever felt misunderstood due to cultural differences in communication?

Values and beliefs: What values and beliefs from my culture significantly influence my communication style? How do I navigate situations where my cultural communication preferences might differ from others?

CHAPTER 6

Time, Time, Time

———

Never do today what you can put off till tomorrow. Delay
may give clear light as to what is best to be done.
—AARON BURR

My father was always habitually late. No matter where we
were going, he was always late. I remember always being
embarrassed about his lateness and amazed to see how calm
he was about it. I cringe as I enter the room if I am running
late. My father? He smiles and greets everyone as if he is
thirty minutes early. Growing up, I had no concept of culture
or how it impacted human behavior. As I grew older and
became exposed to other cultures, I realized that people in
certain cultures can be habitually late, while those from others can be habitually punctual. Much to my dismay, I found
those comfortable being habitually late tend to demonstrate
a laissez-faire attitude while smiling their way into the room.
Alternatively, those who are chronically punctual stress the
importance of being more and more timely. What gives? This
tendency caused considerable conflict and confusion for me.

Ever notice how time never stops ticking? We all experience it, but how we relate to it is super personal and often shaped by our culture.

Imagine you've landed this incredible job as an analyst. You're based in the US, but your company's in Mexico City. Plus, you're fluent in English and Spanish, so you feel like you've got this. Sounds exciting, right?

But here's the twist: Your manager, who's in Mexico, has a way of making things, well, a bit awkward. He's always late for your meetings. Not just once, but every single time. And he never even acknowledges it. Oh, and he's quite interested in your personal life too. It's not just odd. It's starting to feel downright intrusive.

You're left scratching your head. Is this a cultural thing you don't understand? Or is it just him? What do you do now? Do you just grin and bear it, or do you say something? Maybe you should wait for the review process, or perhaps you should bring it up privately.

This is more than a minor annoyance. It's becoming a real crossroads for you, which could make or break your relationship with your supervisor and potentially your career.

What would you do if you were in this situation? It's a tricky situation, isn't it? One where understanding cultural differences isn't just a nicety. It's a must if you navigate this new world without stepping on any landmines.

How we handle time, communicate, and even get personal can vary wildly from culture to culture. And in a world without borders, where we're all working together, understanding these nuances is more than just good manners. It's essential to work better together.

EMILY

Emily is full of charm and ambition, and like many of us, she faces a time-oriented clash when she moves to Paris (Fleming 2020).

Emily comes from Chicago, where time is money and the clock is always ticking. Her bread and butter is her nine-to-five grind, punctual meetings, and tight deadlines. But Paris? Well, that's a whole different ball game.

Imagine Emily's shock when she discovers her new French colleagues have a laissez-faire approach to time. Showing up fashionably late is the norm, and lunches stretch on in a delightful, leisurely fashion. It's not about rushing from one task to another. It's about savoring the moment. Can you picture Emily's wide-eyed surprise? Maybe you've felt that way yourself in a new environment. I certainly have.

At first, Emily is like a fish out of water. She's the early bird, waiting for her colleagues, who stroll in at their own pace. She's eager to wrap up lunches quickly, while everyone else seems content to chat away. In her mind, she's playing the beat of efficiency, but the French dance to a tempo of pleasure and enjoyment (Fleming 2020). Can you relate to that sense of confusion? That feeling like everyone knows the dance moves, but you?

But Emily is no quitter. She starts to observe, learn, and even embrace this new pace. She sees these long lunches are not just about food but about connections, conversations, and a shared sense of community. It's not about being late or procrastinating. It's about valuing quality over quantity and creativity over rigid timelines.

There's this one scene where Emily starts to "get it." Spoiler alert: Emily gets fired from both jobs. She doesn't just rush to get another job. She decides to take a brief hiatus and enjoy the city. Suddenly, she's not watching the clock (Fleming 2020).

She's enjoying lunch with Luc by the Roue de Paris (Fleming 2020). She's present, absorbed in the moment, and it clicks. It's not about losing time. It's about gaining relationships and enjoying life. It's a "Eureka!" moment we can all appreciate.

Throughout her Parisian journey, Emily doesn't just survive; she thrives. She balances her hardwired American punctuality with the French love for the present moment. And in doing so, she's more than an effective worker. She's a more complete person (Fleming 2020).

Emily's story is not just about adjusting to a work environment. It's about understanding a new way of life. Her story is about adapting, not adopting. It's a lesson in flexibility and the importance of tuning in to different cultural beats without losing your rhythm. Emily reminds us it's not always about the race against the clock. Sometimes, it's about slowing down, embracing a different pace, and finding joy in the journey. All without losing ourselves in the process (Fleming 2020).

So, next time you find yourself rushing through lunch or getting impatient with someone's different sense of time, remember Emily. Maybe, just maybe, there's a lesson in there for all of us. What do you think?

I've had exciting experiences with colleagues from different cultures regarding managing our time during meetings. One time, we were trying to plan out a strategy session and figure out how long each part should take. I was trying to schedule everything out precisely, but my colleagues pushed back and said we didn't need to stick to a strict schedule. Ultimately, each part of the meeting exceeded the allotted time, and our agenda was more of a souvenir. This happens a lot in workplaces worldwide and those in our backyard. For example, Western cultures tend to focus on deadlines and urgent tasks, while other cultures might see time as more flexible and less predictable. Cultures that use polychronic time often have a more easy-going attitude toward managing time.

POLY-*WHAT*?

Ever notice how some people seem super focused on doing one thing at a time while others are juggling a dozen things all at once? In his book *Beyond Culture*, Edward Hall cracked the code on cultural timekeeping.

Picture your friend from Switzerland who's all about precision. If you've ever tried to get their attention while they're on the phone, you've probably been met with a "hold on" gesture. They're in what Hall calls the monochronic zone, where time is a straight line and multitasking is a no-go (Hall 1977, 74).

Now, think of your Italian friend who's the exact opposite. They're thriving while they have the phone in one hand, a coffee in the other, and probably cooking dinner simultaneously. They live in a polychronic time, where life's unpredictable, and the more you can juggle, the better (Hall 1977, 74).

Some people stick to the clock like glue, while others are more fluid, going with the flow. Think about how you prefer to text or email your friends. Some of you might like rapid-fire texting. Others prefer a slow and thoughtful email. That's the difference between cultures that thrive on speed and efficiency and value relationships and connections over quick replies.

What's interesting about all of this is how our approach to time tells a story about what we value in ways that may distort how we are perceived. And if you're not careful, these differences in time management preferences can make working with diverse people a real rollercoaster.

So, back to our Italian friend. They've got this multitasking thing down to an art form. They're not just juggling their day but putting on a whole circus performance. This way of handling time might feel alien to some, but it may make them super adaptable to change.

On the flip side, our Swiss friend with the one-track mind might see time as precision. They're all about punctuality, following agendas, and getting things done in a straight line. A random coffee break or casual chitchat? Is it on the calendar?

Some might call this multitasking ability a blessing, while others might call it a severe ADD case like mine. But no judgment here! These differences in time management preferences might seem small, but they can make a world of difference when working with different people. Someone used to a monochronic way of life, where time is strictly scheduled, might feel thrown off and even a bit uncomfortable in a polychronic culture, where time is more fluid and less precise. Businesses that measure the success of a project by how promptly objectives are met might need help to keep their concerns at bay when working with overseas partners who follow a more flexible, polychronic approach to time. Conversely, those accustomed to the polychronic way might have difficulty connecting with monochronic partners, often feeling the relationship is too stiff, formal, or even distant (Trompenaars and Woolliams 2003, 597).

Whether it's being able to switch apps and keep a conversation going in a meeting (like our friends in Latin America, the Middle East, or Southern Europe) or staying focused on one task at a time (like our friends in the United States, Canada, or Germany) understanding how different cultures dance with time is like having a secret key to unlock better relationships and teamwork (Trompenaars and Woolliams 2003, 603).

So next time you find yourself baffled by someone's approach to time, remember—it may not be them. It's culture. And knowing how to navigate those cultural rhythms is a skill worth its weight in gold (or, in the case of our Italian friend, probably espresso!).

SHORT-TERM VERSUS LONG-TERM ORIENTATION

Geert Hofstede's research on cultural dimensions has taught us a lot about how people from different cultures communicate and behave (Hofstede, Hofstede, and Minkov 2010, 273). The idea of short-term and long-term orientation is fascinating because it shows us how different cultures view time and how it affects their emotions and communication. Hofstede's work highlights how different cultures approach communication, relationships, and time, which is still relevant today.

According to Hofstede, Hofstede, and Minkov, societies can be categorized into short-term and long-term (2010, 273). Short-term cultures may value efficiency and time-saving methods, prioritizing the present and immediate future. These societies may be open to taking risks and promoting innovation. On the other hand, long-term cultures tend to value following rules and respecting authority figures, prioritizing the future. People in these societies may have a strong sense of duty and commitment to group harmony.

If you're a manager, it's essential to understand the cultural perspective of your team members so you can communicate effectively and help them reach their goals. And if you're an individual contributor, understanding where your colleagues and boss are coming from may help you work together smoothly.

LONG-TERM ORIENTATION

Thinking ahead and long-term planning is what having a long-term orientation is all about. It means prioritizing future success over immediate gratification, which may require sacrificing short-term rewards from time to time (Hofstede, Hofstede, and Minkov 2010, 273).

Having a long-term preference at work may represent focusing on the larger goals. Instead of seeking instant gratification, you may prioritize long-lasting achievements. Being patient and willing to delay short-term gains for greater success in the future is crucial. Additionally, perseverance and a strong work ethic may assist in overcoming the obstacles and intricacies of planning for the future. Your determination to succeed in long-term goals may be your focus.

In your personal life, you may invest in education and skill-building, knowing that these investments may not pay off immediately but will provide opportunities for career advancement and financial stability. You may focus on careful budgeting and saving for future needs, such as buying a house, retirement, or a child's education, rather than spending on immediate desires and luxuries. Your personal relationships might involve investing time and energy in building deep and meaningful connections with family and friends, recognizing that these relationships provide enduring support and fulfillment. Your long-term health may be the focus, emphasizing practices that promote wellness, such as regular exercise, healthy eating, and preventative health-care measures. You may invest in ongoing self-improvement, seek out new learning opportunities, and set personal growth goals that align with long-term visions. In parenting, you may focus on instilling values, ethics, and skills to help children grow into responsible and successful adults rather than addressing immediate behavior or short-term challenges.

SHORT-TERM ORIENTATION

If you have a short-term orientation preference, you may focus on the past and present rather than the future (Hofstede, Hofstede, and Minkov 2010, 273). Maybe you value following traditions, keeping your social obligations, and fulfilling your responsibilities. You may find happiness in short-term gratification rather than working toward long-term goals. In the workplace, this short-term approach may represent a preference for projects that produce quick results, leading to impatience with longer-term endeavors.

In our personal lives, we may prioritize our short-term desires over our long-term goals. We might spend impulsively on gadgets and vacations without thinking much about our financial future. Or we might make health choices based on immediate pleasure rather than long-term well-being, such as indulging in unhealthy foods or avoiding exercise. In relationships, we may give precedence to immediate satisfaction over long-term plans. Even our education and career choices can be influenced by short-term gains rather than aligning with our long-term aspirations. As parents, we may focus on addressing immediate behavior challenges rather than instilling long-term values and habits in our children. While satisfying our immediate needs may feel good, it can lead to challenges in the future if we neglect mindful long-term planning and growth.

SAM

Sam is an exceptionally talented programmer. His colleagues have always admired his abilities to solve complex problems and design innovative solutions. Sam also happens to be neurodiverse, diagnosed with Asperger's syndrome. He thrives on structure and consistency, especially regarding time management. He prefers clear instructions and schedules and adheres to them meticulously. In his mind, time is almost a sacred construct, and punctuality is nonnegotiable.

"Structure helps me stay organized and work better," he said.

Sam's new leader, Clara, comes from a fluid culture where relationships take precedence. Clara approaches her work with flexibility and spontaneity. She often adjusts meetings at the last minute, extending discussions if they engage and weaving in personal stories and connection-building questions.

The time orientation clash between Sam and Clara becomes apparent almost immediately. Sam is frustrated and anxious by Clara's lackadaisical approach to structure and schedule, and Clara is equally confused by Sam's rigidity.

"I couldn't understand why she keeps changing things without reason," he explained. "The way she does things is very frustrating!"

Sam becomes visibly distressed during team meetings when discussions go off the agenda, or Clara spontaneously reschedules. On the other hand, Clara feels restricted by Sam's insistence on sticking strictly to the plan and his reluctance to engage in more casual, relationship-building conversations.

"She is always asking me about my personal life, which has nothing to do with my work," he told me.

"One day, she asked for my opinion about an upcoming meeting. I was surprised but gave her some tips on running effective meetings."

Clara takes the initiative to understand Sam better. She learns about neurodiversity and realizes his need for structure and predictability isn't just a preference—it's essential for his well-being and productivity.

Simultaneously, Sam opens up about his needs and why structure is vital. He is also willing to understand Clara's approach, acknowledging that her relational style has merits.

Clara and Sam agree on a compromise. Clara begins to give Sam more advanced notice if meetings are to be rescheduled and ensures that agendas are followed as closely as possible. She also sets aside time for relationship-building without infringing on Sam's need for structure and privacy.

Sam, in turn, makes an effort to engage more personally with Clara, understanding that this connection is valuable to her. He finds that brief one-on-one interactions, where the environment is more controlled, allow him to connect without feeling overwhelmed.

Through understanding, empathy, communication, and mutual respect, Clara and Sam build a working relationship that honors both their cultural values and Sam's neurodiversity. They discovered how to use their differences to connect better.

Sam and Clara highlight the potential magic that happens when leaders and team members take the time to understand and accommodate each other's unique preferences, backgrounds, and needs. They create a more inclusive environment and enable more effective collaboration. Recognizing the richness in our differences and navigating them with empathy, we can turn potential challenges into opportunities for growth and connection. In this case, Clara led the way in connecting with Sam. Leading understanding and empathy helped Clara meet Sam where he was, which increased his willingness to participate.

Figuring out how we view time isn't just some brainy thought experiment. It's a real deep dive into what makes us tick (pun intended!). It can change how we live, relate to others, and what we go after in life. Some of us may be all about what's happening right now, while others may always look ahead to what's next. This view of time shapes our decisions and paths, leaving a mark on our lives that is as individual as our fingerprints. It's something that sticks with us, and it's as real and lasting as time itself. How's that for something to think about next time you check your watch?

How do our cultural values shape the way we view authority? Join me as we venture into authority central.

PERSPECTIVE

Understanding your time orientation and how it aligns with your cultural preferences can provide valuable insights into your behavior and decision-making processes. Reflecting on the following questions might help you explore this aspect of yourself.

Prioritization: How do you prioritize your daily tasks and long-term goals? Do you focus more on immediate needs or future planning?

Decision-making: When faced with a choice, do you tend to make decisions that gratify immediate desires, or do you consider the long-term consequences?

Relationships: Think about your relationships with friends and family. Do you seek immediate connections and satisfaction, or do you invest time in building deep, lasting relationships?

Work ethics: In your career, are you driven more by immediate achievements and recognition or by long-term success and growth?

Financial management: How do you manage your finances? Are you inclined to spend on immediate pleasures, or do you save and invest for future needs?

Health choices: Reflect on your daily health habits. Do you make choices that feel good in the moment, or do you follow a regimen that will benefit you in the long run?

Education and personal growth: Think about your educational and personal growth paths. Are you drawn to quick gains and interests, or do you choose paths that align with your long-term goals?

Environmental responsibility: How do you make choices regarding the environment? Do you prioritize convenience and personal benefit, or do you think about long-term sustainability?

Parenting (If applicable): If you are a parent, do you focus more on addressing immediate behavior challenges or on nurturing the long-term values and habits you want to instill in your children?

Recreational choices: Consider your hobbies and leisure activities. Do you prioritize immediate fun and entertainment or engage in activities that align with your broader life goals and values?

Cultural influences: How has your cultural background and upbringing shaped your time orientation? Do cultural norms or values influence how you perceive and manage time?

Challenges and adaptation: Have you ever faced challenges due to your time orientation preferences? How have you adapted or changed to align with different cultural or personal contexts?

CHAPTER 7

Just Tell Me What to Do

---

*The more I learn about other cultures, the more I learn that
I need to know more about my own culture.*
—*AISTE PTAKAUSKE, EDUCATOR*

I was sitting in my office chair, feeling like a total idiot.
"Why?" I often wondered. Why are topics always addressed
to me when my staff is more than capable of addressing any
topic? For example, why were they calling me about a meeting that needed to be canceled when the person leading the
meeting was one of my staff members, albeit of a lower rank?

Another example I recall is the need for all approvals to come
from department heads, regardless of how small the matter or expenditure is. Needs to be more agile, right? Well, it
depends on who you ask. My version of agility was based on
North American leadership ideals, which are very different
in different cultures, especially across Latin America, Asia,
and Western Europe.

My preferred leadership style is diplomatic, where everyone strives together to get results. I always thought I was an effective leader who empowered team members to address matters independently and escalate as needed. However, when I began managing diverse local or global teams, I noticed my leadership style was less effective than I thought.

Employees who preferred high power distance had a defined yet implied expectation of how to be managed. They expected to be directed and told what to do with little room for deference. I noticed it at home too. Elders were sacred not only because of their wisdom but because of their hierarchical standing in the family. Employees who preferred a low power-distance approach were comfortably aligned with my preferred leadership style.

Power distance, a cultural dimension developed by Geert Hofstede, refers to the extent to which less powerful members of a society accept that power is distributed unequally (2010, 61). It's not just an academic concept. It has profound and tangible effects on everyday interactions at work and in social settings.

HIGH POWER-DISTANCE

In cultures with high power distance, you'll often find strict hierarchies and clear distinctions between social classes, age groups, and professional ranks. Let's say you're an employee who values high power distance. You might hesitate to speak up during meetings or offer feedback to superiors. This isn't necessarily because you're shy or lacking in insight. It may be because your cultural preferences discourage such "insubordination." In these societies, parents, teachers, and bosses may often viewed as unquestionable authority figures, making it difficult for younger generations or subordinates to voice different perspectives or innovate. This may stifle creativity and lead to a lack of accountability among those in power (Hofstede, Hofstede, and Minkov 2010, 61). In a high power-distance family, elders command enormous respect, and their word is often law (Hofstede, Hofstede, and Minkov 2010, 61).

LOW POWER-DISTANCE

In low power-distance cultures, on the other hand, equality and decentralized authority are prized. Subordinates are encouraged to speak up, and hierarchies are less rigid. This may cultivate a culture of innovation but may lead to conflicts and less clarity in roles if not well-managed. In social interactions, low power distance often manifests as a strong sense of egalitarianism. Family dynamics also differ based on power-distance values. Elders might be respected, but they're not necessarily seen as infallible or untouchable.

POWER DISTANCE IN ACTION

Power distance isn't just a corporate term. It's something we encounter daily, affecting how we interact with family, friends, and strangers. Have you ever felt uncomfortable calling your friend's parents by their first names? That's power distance. Are you hesitant to question your older sibling's advice even when disagreeing? Yep, power distance again. This invisible hierarchy influences whom we listen to, make decisions, and even see ourselves concerning others. Understanding it can help us navigate tricky social dynamics, find our voice, and build more equitable relationships. In high power-distance families, younger family members may be expected to adhere to traditional roles and customs without question, which may provide a structured environment but may suppress individual expression. In low power-distance families, relationships tend to be more egalitarian, leading to greater role flexibility and unrestricted exchange of ideas. This can result in more freedom for individual expression but may sometimes mean elders are not given the respect or care customary in high power-distance settings.

Even the patient-doctor relationship varies. In a high power-distance culture, patients are less likely to question a doctor's advice, seek a second opinion, or advocate for themselves, possibly leading to less-than-ideal healthcare outcomes. In low power-distance cultures, the healthcare experience is often more collaborative but can also lead to "over-shopping" for medical advice, causing delays in treatment. In high power-distance cultures, patients might not question a doctor's diagnosis or prescribed treatment, putting them at potential risk if the doctor errs. Students in high power-distance cultures might memorize facts but hesitate to engage in critical thinking or debate with authority figures for fear of contradicting the teacher.

Power distance subtly yet significantly shapes our day-to-day interactions and experiences, influencing our respect for authority, willingness to speak up, approach to conflict, and how we seek and provide care. It's a ubiquitous cultural metric that informs our subliminal expectations, dictating how we relate to others and, more importantly, how we expect others to relate to us. Understanding its implications can help us navigate the complexities of both our personal and professional lives.

The ripple effects go even further. In high power-distance societies, there can be a greater acceptance of inequalities, leading to less pressure on governments to enact policies that reduce social disparities. In low power-distance societies, there might be a stronger push for policies that level the playing field. Still, it may also lead to a discounting of expertise, as everyone's opinion is considered equally valid.

Navigating these waters becomes tricky in our globalized world, where high and low power-distance cultures often converge. The ability to understand and adapt to different cultural values—known as cultural intelligence—becomes crucial here. Being aware of power-distance orientations can help us adapt our communication styles, manage teams effectively, and build stronger relationships both in and outside the workplace. It can also help us reflect on our deeply ingrained beliefs about power and authority and how they influence our interactions with others.

Understanding the concept of power distance and its effects on daily life enables us to appreciate the nuances of cultural interaction. It also equips us with the tools to navigate these complex dynamics more effectively, whether we're closing a business deal, discussing a grade with a teacher, or even understanding national politics.

JACK

Jack, a seasoned baby boomer with thirty years of experience in the tech industry, reports to Lisa, a millennial who has been in the workforce for less than a decade. At first, the power distance between them feels like a chasm. Jack is used to hierarchical structures, where bosses give orders and subordinates follow. On the other hand, Lisa encourages open dialogue and teamwork and dislikes top-down management.

Initially, this generational gap is a source of tension. Jack feels uncomfortable speaking freely in team meetings, worried it may seem like he's overstepping his boundaries. He hesitates to offer input on new projects, not wanting to appear to be challenging Lisa's authority. Lisa senses this hesitation but mistakes it for disinterest or, even worse, condescension.

Things reach a breaking point during a team meeting where Lisa proposes a new approach to software development. Sensing Jack's reservation, she asks him point-blank what his thoughts are. After an uncomfortable pause, Jack finally speaks, "In my experience, the methods we have been using have proven effective. This new approach could be more of a risk."

Lisa feels criticized but remembers a seminar she took on managing across generations. She takes a deep breath and says, "I appreciate your experience, Jack, and I think it's crucial for our team's success. How about we do a small-scale test run of the new approach and evaluate its effectiveness?"

Feeling acknowledged, Jack agrees. During the test run, Jack leans into his curiosity, recognizing that he can learn something valuable from this younger generation's approach to problem-solving and adaptability. He observes how open Lisa is to feedback and how she's willing to pivot when things aren't working, qualities he admires.

The trial is a mixed bag—some things work, some don't, but the approach shows promise. Jack feels far more comfortable providing his thoughts in the follow-up meeting, blending his tried-and-true experience with Lisa's innovative methods. The balance is suddenly harmonious, almost symbiotic.

Over time, Jack starts to appreciate Lisa's inclusive leadership style, and Lisa gains a deeper respect for Jack's experience. Jack finds the reduced power distance emphasis makes the office a more enjoyable, collaborative environment, making him more productive and fulfilled. Lisa also realizes that Jack's depth of knowledge can serve as a foundation upon which to build new strategies.

Though it takes time, the two form an unlikely yet powerful partnership. They see that although they come from different generations, their diverse perspectives are not a hindrance but an asset. And it all starts with the willingness to close the gap, to meet in the middle, effectively tearing down the invisible but palpable power-distance walls.

So there you have it: power distance is more than just some abstract, stuffy concept discussed in boardrooms or sociology classes. It's the invisible puppeteer pulling the strings in your everyday interactions, from awkward family dinners to who takes charge of a group project. Understanding power distance is your cheat sheet if you've ever felt like a contestant in the *Who's the Boss?* game show of life. Use it wisely, navigate it respectfully, and the next time someone tries to pull rank on you, you'll be armed with more understanding.

Do cultural values influence how we build trust? Let's turn the page and find out.

PERSPECTIVE

These questions cultivate a deeper understanding of how power distance can shape interactions, expectations, and behaviors in different scenarios.

Audit your cultural preferences: How does your cultural background shape your perception of authority figures like bosses, teachers, or elders? Can you think of a specific situation where your views on power distance clashed with someone else's expectations in daily life?

Navigating diverse teams: Imagine you're a manager in a multinational corporation. You've got a team of people from high and low power-distance cultures. How would you approach delegation, feedback, and team meetings to ensure everyone's cultural preferences around power distance are respected?

Step into the classroom: Put yourself in the shoes of a student in a high power-distance culture. How might your classroom experience differ from that of a student in a low power-distance culture? How would this affect your willingness to ask questions, challenge viewpoints, or seek clarification?

Consider healthcare settings: If you were a patient in a high power-distance culture, would you feel comfortable questioning a doctor's diagnosis or treatment plan? What if you were in a low power-distance culture? Would your approach change? Why or why not?

Reflect on family dynamics: If you grew up in a low power-distance household, how might your experience and relationship with your parents differ from someone who grew up in a high power-distance environment? How do these early life experiences influence how you navigate relationships and authority in your day-to-day adult life?

CHAPTER 8

Is Trust Universal?

Trust starts with truth and ends with truth. Without trust,
we don't truly collaborate; we merely coordinate or, at best,
cooperate. It is trust that transforms a group of people into
a team.

—STEVEN COVEY, SPEED OF TRUST

"I would invite you to lunch, but I know you will say no," she
told me.

"Thank you. I'll see you when you get back," I replied.

"Why don't you come with us?"

I always thought of something to say that was socially
accepted. Or so I thought.

I'm an introvert. This was yet another invitation I declined.
I'm busy—too many things to do. There's always a priority
somewhere, and results must be obtained. Raised with an
understanding that emotions are not expressed openly and

trust is earned through competency, reliability, and results, all my personal and professional relationships were perceived through this lens.

Trust is vital in any relationship, especially in the workplace. It makes employees feel seen, heard, and like they belong. A quick search on Google for "psychological safety" brings up about 53,400,000 results, while "trust" has an impressive 628,000,000 results. But what does trust represent? Building trust is vital, but it can be tricky in a diverse world, especially in virtual spaces where global is now local. Trust has to be earned. It can't just be given. It can be influenced by cultural values shaped by local, regional, national, and international experiences (Van Dyne et al. 2000, 8).

I never experienced this more than when I began working in a globally multicultural setting. I quickly learned that cultural values influence how we prefer and expect to build trust.

Cultural values are as significant in the context of global interactions and multicultural workplaces as they are locally. They profoundly influence local, regional, and national societies. The societal norms, communication styles, work ethics, and educational systems within a city, region, or country reflect its unique cultural value tapestry. Think of a small town where everyone knows everyone and mutual aid is a common practice—a classic sign of a collective culture. Or consider a buzzing city where independence and individual achievement are celebrated, indicative of an individualistic culture. Cultural values can shape the social dynamics, decision-making processes, and even the political leanings of a society, whether it's a rural community, a sprawling city, a geographical region, or an entire nation. These unique cultural nuances give each place its character, personality, and distinct identity.

When I started my career in a mono-cultural environment, my management style was about competition, individual success, and getting results. However, I soon realized building trust in multicultural environments requires a different approach. Despite using the usual pleasantries through friendly greetings like "hello," I found they were insufficient to build deeper connections in different cultures, especially relationship-driven ones.

One approach to building relationships may not be appropriate in a different culture or context. Results-driven cultures like mine cultivate trust through reliance, results, and success. On the other hand, relationship-driven cultures may cultivate trust through relationships, loyalty, and dependability (Van Dyne et al. 2000, 8).

HOW OUR CULTURAL VALUES INFLUENCE OUR PERCEPTION OF TRUST

Imagine you're navigating the world with a unique trust-building blueprint in your mind. The blueprint has no geographical boundaries. It can be local as it can be global. This blueprint isn't static but is shaped and reshaped by your cultural context—your society's unwritten rules and tacit understandings about how people should behave. Just as these cultural values influence our approach to work, communication, and social interactions, they also profoundly affect how we interact and develop trust.

Bear in mind these cultural dimensions are spectrums, not absolutes. They offer clues to navigate the trust-building labyrinth but are not a one-size-fits-all map. Now, dig into these cultural blueprints and see how diverse cultural values impact trust building.

First, let's talk about communication style, which can be high or low-context. Picture this: You're meeting a new business associate for the first time. If you come from a high-context culture, trust begins with the subtleties—the shared experiences, the nonverbal cues, the hints hidden between the lines. In contrast, if you're from a low-context culture, you trust clear, direct, and explicit expressions. It's like the difference between reading a poem versus a user manual.

John, an accountant native of the Midwest, grew up in a low-context culture. He learned early on that he prefers to build trust by expressing himself directly and values clear communication. He tends to be transparent and upfront about his intentions and expects the same straightforwardness from others. On the other hand, Maria Jose, a Latin American IT consultant who identifies as a woman, comes from a high-context culture, where more is conveyed through nonverbal cues and indirect communication. She builds trust by recognizing and responding to these subtleties and expects others to do the same.

Next, we have power distance, the degree to which less powerful members of a society accept power inequality. In high power-distance cultures, trust often mirrors a waterfall cascading from the top down. In contrast, in low power-distance cultures, trust resembles a calm lake built on equality, involvement, and open dialogue. Susan, a tech entrepreneur in Silicon Valley, comes from a culture that values low power distance. She encourages an egalitarian environment where everyone has a say. Susan builds trust by involving her team in decision-making and expects employees to speak up and participate actively.

In contrast, Andrew, the CEO of a family business in New Jersey, comes from a high power distance background. He values hierarchy and builds trust by showing strong leadership and making informed decisions. Andrew expects his employees to trust his judgment and follow his lead without question.

Now, consider uncertainty avoidance, the extent to which a society feels uncomfortable with uncertainty and ambiguity. If you prefer a culture with high uncertainty avoidance, you might find trust in clear rules, consistent behavior, and the comforting glow of predictability. On the flip side, if you thrive in low uncertainty avoidance environments, trust might be rooted in adaptability, innovation, and the courage to navigate the unpredictable.

Lina is a New York-based financial analyst who appreciates structure and predictability, indicative of high uncertainty avoidance. She builds trust by being consistent, reliable, and following established rules. Lina expects others to adhere to these same rules and standards.

On the flip side, Ben, an innovator from California, is comfortable with ambiguity, a characteristic of low uncertainty avoidance cultures. He builds trust through being adaptable, encouraging creativity, and gracefully navigating uncertain situations. Ben expects others to be open to change and adapt quickly to new circumstances.

The next stop in our trust-building journey is the individualism/collectivism dimension. Trust is often anchored in personal credibility and direct relationships in individualistic cultures. But for collectivist cultures, trust is based on a reputation handed down from your group or community. It's like the difference between being vouched for by your past achievements versus being vouched for by your family's or group's standing.

Richard, an independent consultant from Chicago, represents an individualistic culture. He builds trust through personal credibility, demonstrated competency, and honoring commitments that get results. Richard expects others to be self-reliant and uphold their promises to get results.

Conversely, Nina, whose parents immigrated from Italy, a collectivist society, values community ties. She builds trust by being a team player, supporting her colleagues, and upholding her group's reputation. Nina expects others to respect and value the team over individual gains.

Moving forward, let's explore the neutral versus affective dimension. Trust might feel like a well-oiled machine in neutral cultures—built by consistency, reliability, and competence. But trust may feel like a heartfelt melody in affective cultures—fueled by expressed emotions and personal connections. It's the difference between trusting a reliable brand and a friend's passionate recommendation.

Sophia, a Miami-based event planner of Colombian descent, values an affective culture. Her approach to trust-building is centered around personal connections, warm interactions, and open expression of emotions. Sophia builds trust by genuinely caring for others, sharing personal stories, and expressing her feelings. She expects others to reciprocate these feelings, and she values emotional sincerity. She is contrasted with George, a scientist in a Boston-based lab, who represents a neutral culture. For him, trust is built through demonstrated competence, consistency, and reliability rather than overt emotional expressions. George prefers a more reserved, formal approach and values logic and facts over emotions. He expects others to build trust through professional competence and deliver on their commitments.

The long-term versus short-term orientation continuum also influences how we perceive and build trust. Trust is like a majestic tree for long-term oriented cultures, growing slowly over time, nurtured by perseverance and the accumulation of mutual respect. But trust might be a flash of fireworks in short-term oriented cultures—quick results and immediate rapport that ignite trust. It's the contrast between a slow-burning candle and a sparkler. Jessica, a California tech startup manager, embodies the short-term orientation common in many fast-paced, results-oriented business environments in the US. She builds trust by demonstrating quick results, solving immediate challenges, and building rapport quickly. Jessica expects others to deliver immediate results, respond swiftly to changes, and maintain a similar pace.

Conversely, Chen, an engineer whose parents emigrated from China, a culture with a more long-term orientation, brings a different perspective to his role in a Detroit manufacturing company. He builds trust through the steady accumulation of mutual respect, reliability, and proven competence over time. Chen values patience, long-term planning, and sustainable solutions. He expects others to demonstrate the same consistency, perseverance, and commitment to the long term.

Lastly, let's look at the being versus doing dimension. If you're from a "doing" culture, the trust could be akin to a to-do list—earned through accomplishments, actions, and results. But in "being" cultures, trust might feel like a reflection in a still pond—about who you are, your character, and your connections. It's like trusting someone who consistently delivers versus someone who makes you feel valued and understood. Jennifer, a counselor from Seattle, is from a "being" culture. She builds trust by being empathetic, understanding, and forming genuine connections. Jennifer expects others to be genuine, present, and emotionally available. On the flip side, James, an investment banker in Boston, originates from a "doing" culture. He builds trust through actions, results, and performance. James expects others to deliver on their commitments and demonstrate competence.

TRUST AT WORK

We carry our cultural blueprints wherever we go, and they are particularly influential in our workplaces. Cultural values can shape our actions and expectations at work in many ways. Understanding these differences helps us navigate the complexities of our multicultural workplaces and build stronger, more effective relationships and teams (Hofstede, Hofstede, and Minkov 2010, 122). Let's explore some examples of how these cultural values can play out in a professional environment:

Communication - Let's say you're launching a new project. In a high-context culture, you might begin by recounting a relevant personal story or sharing an anecdote about a similar project. Accustomed to reading between the lines, your team will pick up on your message and understand your expectations. However, in a low-context culture, your team would likely appreciate a straightforward briefing detailing what's needed and when.

Decision-making - Consider a situation where your organization needs to make a critical decision. In a high power-distance culture, the senior management will most likely make the decision, and employees would generally accept this as the norm. However, in a low power-distance culture, you might find an open discussion where everyone, regardless of rank, is invited to share their thoughts and opinions before deciding.

Uncertainty avoidance - Imagine you're introducing a new business process. In a high uncertainty avoidance culture, employees would appreciate detailed instructions, frequent updates, and support during the transition. In a low uncertainty avoidance culture, employees might be comfortable with a high-level overview and the autonomy to figure out the details themselves.

Performance management - Suppose there's a performance issue with a team in your organization. If you have high individualistic preferences, you'd likely have a private conversation with the person responsible. However, if you have high collectivist preferences, the issue might be addressed as a general topic with the whole team, emphasizing collective responsibility and improvement.

Relationships - In a neutral culture, employees might build trust by showing up on time, meeting deadlines, and doing quality work. In an affective culture, trust might be made through after-work socializing, sharing personal stories, or showing empathy in the workplace.

Negotiations - In a business negotiation, a long-term-oriented culture might place a high value on building a strong relationship before sealing the deal. They may take time to get to know their potential partners, seeking mutual benefits for the future. On the other hand, a short-term-oriented culture might be more focused on the immediate benefits of the deal, looking for quick results and prompt decision-making.

Recognition - Recognition in a "doing" culture, performance metrics, accomplishments, and the ability to meet targets would likely be the primary considerations. In contrast, in a "being" culture, promotions might be influenced by an individual's character, relationships, and potential for growth.

Between the increasingly virtual world and diverse family dynamics, the time for cultural intelligence and humility is now. Trust may be universal, but the *way* we perceive and build trust differs for different people. Some like building trust through relationships shaped by character and connections, while others like establishing trust through results and deliverables.

Fusing emotional and Social Intelligence with Cultural Intelligence and Cultural Humility cultivates our global citizenship. Focusing on our humanity helps us build trust appropriately for the culture we are working in or relating with to avoid misunderstandings and frustrations. Of course, it is important not to generalize or assume a person's cultural affinity. This is where Social and Emotional Intelligence intersects with Cultural Intelligence and Cultural Humility. Building trust takes time and effort in our personal and professional lives, but it is worth it.

NOT SO BAD

In preparation for this book, I asked a former colleague about her experience working with me before my cultural intelligence journey began. I was relieved I was not as terrible as I thought.

"You always helped me feel seen, heard, and understood," she told me. "Even though you did not understand the culture, you were curious enough to ask questions and always had the grace to accept being wrong."

I was pleased to hear I was not as culturally inept as I thought, even though I crashed a few times. Understanding how cultural values impact trust earned helped me adapt my approach. Since then, I have developed some of the most powerful relationships yet.

Do you ever have conflicts with another person? Let's turn the page and find out how our cultural values shape conflict.

PERSPECTIVE

Understanding how cultural values impact trust development is vital for effective communication and collaboration in our globalized world. Recognizing these nuances fosters respect, minimizes confusion, and promotes inclusivity in various environments. This awareness enhances personal relationships and business interactions across different cultures, making the world a better place.

Friendships: Have you ever considered why your close friend from another culture took a little longer to open up to you? Could it be due to their high-context cultural background, where trust is built slowly over time?

Authority figures and trust: How often have you wondered about the nuances of trust in different cultures? For instance, consider how individuals from high power-distance cultures may equate trust with authority, while those from low power-distance cultures may link it to equality and open dialogue.

Earning trust: Can you recall when someone from a collectivist culture hesitated to trust you until they knew your community or group better?

Trust mismatch: Have you ever experienced a mismatch in building trust with a colleague from a different culture? Could it be a clash between a short-term and long-term orientation?

Perception of emotions: How might you react if someone from an affective culture expressed emotions readily to develop trust while you're more comfortable with a neutral approach?

Professional relationships: How might the "doing" versus "being" cultural dimension impact your professional relationships? Do you find yourself trusting people based on their accomplishments or their character?

Expectations of trust: As you navigate life, consider how uncertainty avoidance might shape your or others' expectations of trust. Is there a preference for clear rules and consistency or flexibility and adaptability?

CHAPTER 9

Why Can't We Just Get Along

———

Getting along with the gang in one place is not any harder than getting along in another. It depends about 98 percent on your own behavior.
—NORMAN VINCENT PEALE

"I don't agree," I explained to a senior executive in Latin America.

Everyone in the meeting was shocked. My American naivete was running the conversation. I did not know why everyone was sitting there silently and visually astonished. We were discussing a new initiative, and I was expressing my disagreement because of the negative impact it was going to have on the employees in the US region.

"Explain," he asked in a very self-managed and gracious tone.

I could tell by his nonverbal behavior that I crossed a line. He came from a high power-distance culture where those in higher ranks did not accept dissent from lower ranks. To make matters worse, my low context and direct communication style prevented me from engaging with the typical pleasantries he was anticipating.

EMILY

When Emily first moves to Paris, she enters a world of new experiences—new job, friends, and culture (Fleming 2020). One of Emily's biggest challenges was navigating conflict resolution, given the stark difference between her American sensibilities and French cultural norms.

During one of her first challenges at work, Emily takes a direct and assertive approach, which is how she would have handled it back home in Chicago. Unfortunately, her French colleagues do not understand this approach, escalating the situation. As a result, Emily's relationships with her new team are negatively impacted (Fleming 2020).

Recognizing her approach isn't working, Emily leans into her cultural intelligence skills. She's driven and motivated to seek perspective by observing her French colleagues like Luc, noting the nuances of their communication and conflict-resolution styles. Following the corporate policy fiasco in episode three of season one, Emily quickly learns that in France, conflicts are often handled more subtly and tactfully, emphasizing dialogue and compromise over direct confrontation. The more Emily learns, the more she adapts her behavior (Fleming 2020).

Applying her newfound understanding, Emily changes her approach. In her next conflict, she engages in a more open, thoughtful conversation, seeking to understand the other person's perspective before asserting her own. She is careful to use diplomacy and respect French discussion etiquette, willing to compromise and find common ground (Fleming 2020).

Emily's adjustment to her conflict resolution style is a turning point. It helps her resolve conflicts more effectively and deepens her relationships at work. She demonstrates that cultural intelligence is about understanding different cultures and applying that understanding to navigate various situations effectively. By doing so, she can bridge the gap between her American values and French norms, enabling her to thrive in her new personal and professional relationship (Fleming 2020).

HOW OUR VALUES SHOW UP IN DIFFERENT AREAS OF CONFLICT

Inevitable conflicts arise in the diverse tapestry of human interaction, but our cultural values determine how we handle them. These values, instilled by our socio-cultural environment, guide our behavior and responses in conflict situations at home and work (Hofstede, Hofstede, and Minkov 2010, 18).

Mark is a tech professional from Silicon Valley who leans toward individualism, a typical cultural value in Western societies like the United States. When confronted with a conflict at work or home, he addresses it directly. He believes in candid communication, asserting his views, and finding a solution through a logical, often competitive, process. His focus is on the problem at hand and the individual responsibilities associated with it.

On the other side of the world, Raj is a senior director at a corporation in India, a culture that strongly values collectivism. Raj prioritizes harmony and group cohesion over individual concerns in conflicts. He opts for indirect communication, employing subtlety and nuance to express dissent. His focus is not just on the immediate problem but on the impact of the conflict on the group's atmosphere and relationships.

Martha, a lawyer from Greece, comes from a high uncertainty avoidance culture. She prefers established procedures, protocols, or legal frameworks to resolve conflicts at home or work, aiming to minimize ambiguity and unpredictability.

On the other side of the spectrum, Mei, a freelance designer from Singapore, comes from a culture with lower uncertainty avoidance. Mei is comfortable with ambiguity and open to exploring innovative solutions when facing conflict. She is willing to negotiate and improvise instead of strictly adhering to rules or formalities.

Miguel, a bank manager from Brazil with a high power-distance culture, defers to the higher ranking roles to resolve conflict situations and respects the decisions made by his elders or superiors.

On the slip side, Jonas, a teacher from Denmark, an extremely low power-distance culture, anticipates conflicts and expects them to be resolved through democratic processes, equal participation, and consensus, regardless of position or status.

Our values, whether at home or work, play a big part in dealing with conflict. They shape our approach, whether direct or indirect, competitive or collaborative, vocal or reserved. In diverse settings, understanding these dynamics can help us appreciate different perspectives and handle conflicts more skillfully.

WHEN CULTURAL VALUES INTERSECT

Of course, our cultural values are not linear and often intersect with other values in ways that may contradict each other to create more opportunities for conflict (Hofstede, Hofstede, and Minkov 2010, 18).

Imagine you're leading a project with a multinational team. You're a doer who likes to get things done efficiently and prefers clear, direct communication. When an issue arises, you address it head-on, laying out the problem and proposing solutions straightforwardly. But your coworkers from "being" and high-context cultures may find this too abrupt. They might prefer to take ample time to understand the situation deeply, discuss it subtly, and not rush toward an immediate solution. What should you do?

Here's another scenario: Let's say you're planning a family reunion with a family that's a blend of low- and high-context cultures. You want to organize everything, make plans, and set a clear agenda—that's your "doing" and low-context approach. But some of your family members from a "being" and high-context culture may feel overwhelmed. They might prefer to enjoy the gathering organically, letting conversations and activities flow naturally rather than sticking to a rigid schedule.

JAKE

Jake is a seasoned sales executive from the heartland of America. He is a charismatic and result-driven individual working in a multinational corporation that's as diverse as it gets. His background predominantly shapes his cultural values, influencing his leadership role.

Raised in an individualistic culture, Jake values autonomy and self-reliance. He believes in the power of competition and sees personal achievement as a measure of success. However, several members of his diverse team, coming from collectivist cultures, value group harmony and collaboration over individual triumph.

Jake is also from a low-context culture where direct, explicit communication is the norm. In contrast, several team members from high-context cultures found his straightforwardness overwhelming. They often misinterpret it as a lack of tact. In addition, Jake comes from a culture with low uncertainty avoidance. He is comfortable with ambiguity and enjoys taking risks in his sales approach. This starkly contrasts some team members from high uncertainty avoidance cultures who prefer predictability and avoid taking undue risks. He struggles to keep the team motivated, which impacts their productivity.

While initially, these differences lead to misunderstandings and tension within the team, Jake's colleagues decide to tap into their cultural intelligence (CQ) to navigate these challenges.

"They were educating me!" he told me about his experience.

Understanding Jake's comfort with direct communication, his colleagues from high-context cultures express their thoughts more explicitly. They acknowledge that in a diverse team, clarity is critical to avoid misunderstandings, even if it means stepping out of their cultural comfort zones.

"Although I travel the world, I was surprised at how much I needed to learn in my backyard," he observed.

For the issues surrounding individualistic versus collectivist perspectives, the team proposes a balanced approach to Jake. They demonstrate how combining the strengths of individual insights with the power of teamwork may lead to innovative solutions and even better sales performance. As a result-oriented person, Jake sees the merit in this approach and is open to integrating more collaborative strategies into his leadership style.

"I figured I needed to meet them halfway," he explained.

To deal with Jake's risk-taking propensity, his risk-averse colleagues initiate discussions about their approach to uncertainty. They explain how their careful planning and risk analysis could also lead to successful sales, albeit less volatile. Jake appreciates this perspective and starts incorporating more structured risk analysis into his strategy.

"I saw how motivated they became when they felt empowered."

Jake's team turned their cultural challenges into strengths through these open conversations and leveraging their CQ. They learn to appreciate each other's differences and develop a more inclusive and effective work environment. The experience teaches Jake that understanding and managing cultural diversity is not a one-person job but a collective effort. When done right, it can pave the way for unparalleled success.

The possible opportunities for conflict are endless. Imagine you're in a relationship with a person from a high-context culture. You disagree with your partner one day and believe in clear communication. You expect your partner to express their feelings and thoughts openly, which is typical in low-context cultures. But your partner might hint at the problem indirectly or stay silent, expecting you to understand the unspoken issue, a common approach in high-context cultures. What should you do?

Both situations reflect cultural values and differences that could lead to misunderstandings and conflicts. Recognizing these differences and finding a balanced approach, a blend of planning and spontaneity or blending direct and indirect communication, could help bridge the gap and lead to more harmonious interactions.

How do you embrace cultural differences to engage more collaboratively? Let's turn the page toward action.

PERSPECTIVE

Reflecting on these prompts can help you better understand your cultural values and their influence on your conflict management style. Recognizing these influences is essential to improving your cultural intelligence and enhancing your interactions with people of diverse backgrounds.

Identify your cultural values: What fundamental values did your culture instill in you? How do these values influence your daily actions, decisions, and interactions?

Reflect on conflict management: How does your culture traditionally handle conflict? Is it common to avoid conflict or to confront it directly? How does this align with your approach?

Understand the influence of cultural values on conflict: Can you recall a situation where your cultural values influenced your reaction to a conflict? How did these values shape your approach?

Analyze cross-cultural conflicts: Have you ever experienced a conflict with someone from a different cultural background? Do you think cultural values played a role in the conflict or its resolution?

Compare conflict resolution styles: Reflect on different styles (avoiding, accommodating, competing, compromising, collaborating). Which one aligns most closely with your culture's approach to conflict?

Explore adaptability in conflict resolution: Have you had to adjust your typical conflict resolution approach when interacting with people from different cultures? How did you navigate these situations?

Seek alternate perspectives: How do other cultures you've encountered approach conflict? What can you learn from these different perspectives?

Consider the impact of cultural values on your relationships: Have your cultural values ever caused misunderstandings or disagreements with others? How did you resolve these?

Examine growth and change: Have your values or approach to conflict evolved due to exposure to different cultures, experiences, or insights? If so, how?

Understanding cultural values involves fostering empathy and appreciation and recognizing that different approaches can be effective in different contexts without labeling them as "better" or "worse."

PART 3

WHERE DO WE GO FROM HERE?

ECHAPTER 10

Knowledge Is Power

I would encourage you: be informed—knowledge is power.
—*MATT BEVIN*

ARROZ CON LECHE

I loved my grandmother's *Arroz con Leche*, a rice pudding made of rice, milk, raisins, and loads of sugar. With each spoon of my grandmother's sweet and creamy arroz con leche, I felt transported to another galaxy with a tender sweetness that can only make a child smile and beg mercilessly for more. Of course, I think back today and wonder why I never went into a diabetic shock! Another favorite dish of mine, *Sancocho*, is a meat stew, including several types of meat and root vegetables like potatoes, yams, and cassava. This soup truly reaches the core of your soul on any day.

The Sancocho is the epitome of all Dominican dishes. It serves multiple purposes in times of peril like illness, joy in celebratory get-togethers, or the go-to recipe for healing a massive hangover. The warmth and comfort I get from eating Sancocho transport me to my days with my grandmother every time I eat it, even today. With each spoon I ingest, I see her smiling at me with joy that still warms my soul. The silky and smooth texture is enough to warm you to the bones on a cold and rainy day.

Mangú, mashed boiled plantains, is another favorite Dominican dish of mine! The creamy and warm texture melts in your mouth as you eat, and it is the perfect companion for any meat, soup, or stew dish. You can eat it for breakfast, lunch, dinner, or alone for an ideal snack. Quipe, not a favorite of mine, is also a traditional Dominican dish (Clara 2023).

Before I understood the intricacies of my Dominican and African heritage, I assumed all the artifacts, cuisine, communication, dances, and other aspects I experienced in Dominican culture originated in the Dominican Republic. Sancocho? Dominican. Mangú? Dominican. Quipe? Dominican…?

Actually, no. Sancocho originated in the Canary Islands, where fish was the only meat used in the recipe. The migration of many Canary Islanders to distinct parts of Latin America, including the Dominican Republic, led to the introduction of this Spanish dish to the region.

The more curious I became about this, the more I learned that many cuisines I presumed had originated in the Dominican Republic originated in Taino, African, Spanish, and Middle Eastern cultures. Arroz con leche originated from Muslim culture and was later introduced to Spain when the Muslims conquered the southern Iberian Peninsula (Empar

2020). While it is a dessert in countries like Spain, Costa Rica, and Peru, it is eaten as a meal in northern Europe. Quipe, another dish widely used in the Dominican Republic and a household staple in my husband's family was introduced to the Dominican Republic by Levantine Lebanese during a migratory wave at the end of the nineteenth century called "Kibbeh" (Clara 2023).

Many foods typical of the Dominican Republic have similarities with those in their sister countries in Latin America. Plantains, white rice, and beans, among others, are common foods throughout Latin America. I always assumed, albeit erroneously, that the foods I unequivocally associated with being Dominican also permeate Latin America.

Interestingly, Cuba, Puerto Rico, and the Dominican Republic claim many dishes, such as tostones. Tostones, the fried green plantain slices that are later flattened and salted, are standard throughout Latin America ("About Tostones"). Mofongo, also popular in the Dominican Republic, is a dish made of fried green plantains or yucca mashed with broth, garlic, oil, and pork cracklings originating in Puerto Rico (Mufarech 2020). Did you know that Mofongo has a fascinating background? It's a dish that combines a mix of cultures, including Spanish, Taíno, African, and North American influences.

Enslaved West Africans introduced fufu to the island, a starchy dish with boiled and pounded plantains, cassava, or yams. Over time, fufu started to include elements of Taíno and Spanish cuisine and eventually became the delicious mofongo we all know and love today (Mufarech 2020).

Mangú, mashed plantains with butter and a bit of milk, is also an African dish made of fufu.

I soon learned these nuances are not limited to cuisine but also influence deep cultural values that impact communication styles, body language, verbal and nonverbal communication, norms, manners, and the concept of family, among others.

KNOWLEDGE AND CULTURE

Before I understood the concept of collectivist cultures, I thought the high emphasis on family and community orientation I was exposed to growing up was also exclusive to Dominican culture. Dominicans are also highly family oriented. Anything, good, bad, or ugly, is always shared with the family. This also meant that personal privacy, space, and boundaries were nonexistent.

Growing up, my mother always made it a point to remind me of this. Her constant reminder to keep my bedroom door open was undoubtedly Dominican. "No cierres la Puerta!" (don't close the door), she would insist. *Whyeeeee?* I wondered. *I need my privacy!* Of course, I only challenged her request in my head, never succumbing to my inner defiance.

Not only was I an introverted kid, I felt that privacy and independence were pivotal aspects of my existence. Boundaries? Nonexistent. I recall often being perceived as antisocial and selfish or a recluse because I enjoyed my quiet moments during social gatherings. Finding a calm space amid a social gathering was considered rude to other family members who wondered, "Que le pása a *ésta* niña?" ("What's wrong with this girl?").

As a second-generation immigrant, I felt compelled to preserve privacy and personal boundaries, even if only in my head! I later learned that perspectives on personal space, privacy, and boundaries are also influenced by culture. Family and the community are at the center of all activities in the Dominican Republic. Sharing celebrations with extended family and neighboring community members is common.

Understanding the different aspects that shape culture helps us understand why different cultures have behaviors and interactions that differ from one another. I always felt personal privacy and space were an existential necessity for me, but it was a faux pas for my mother. Personal privacy, or lack thereof, was another aspect I attributed exclusively to Dominican culture. I later learned that privacy, boundaries, and space are unacknowledged in some cultures while revered in others. In individualistic cultures such as North America, these things are expected, while they may be limited in collectivist cultures like China, Japan, India, and Indonesia (Nakada and Tamura 2005, 31).

Understanding culture at a macro level is an essential precursor to forming appropriate assumptions and judgments about people's behavior in various cultural contexts. It allows you to recognize when your actions are out of place or wrong. A significant part of socializing outside our culture often comes down to assessing how people from other places act in comparison to our customs and adjusting our behavior accordingly.

Acquiring cultural intelligence is essential, and it involves knowing how culture influences people's behavior, beliefs, and thinking patterns. This knowledge has two parts: cultural-general and context-specific understanding (Livermore 2009, 50). Cultural-general understanding means getting a good grasp of the values, beliefs, and norms that are typical in a specific culture. At the same time, context-specific understanding focuses on how culture affects specific areas (Livermore 2009, 50). For example, knowing about a culture's power-distance value can help a manager understand why employees from cultures where power distance is highly valued may tend to let their leader make decisions or a person understand why a family member may not advocate for themselves at the doctor's office.

Whether working with people from different cultures, leading a global team, or navigating cultural value differences within your family, CQ Knowledge is like a well-stocked kitchen spice cabinet, offering various flavors and seasonings that can enrich any dish. Applying cultural intelligence in everyday life means knowing when to use each spice and enhancing interactions and relationships through a deep understanding of diverse cultures and contexts.

There's no single "normal" way of behaving. What may be acceptable in one culture could be perceived as strange or even offensive in another (Livermore 2011, 85)

I learned from my own experiences that I used to focus too much on my goals and didn't think about how my actions affected the group, especially in cultures prioritizing the community over the individual. But if I had known more about how these cultures work toward common goals, I could have earned their trust more quickly. It took me a while to understand I needed to adjust my individualistic tendencies to meet the group's expectations and build a stronger bond.

Navigating the terrain of familial relationships became particularly challenging when my individualistic preferences collided with my collectivist family members. Personal freedom and self-expression have always been a must-have, like an instrumentalist solo in an orchestra. On the other hand, my family operates like a close-knit orchestra, where each instrument's role is clearly defined and contributes to a harmonious melody. Whether choosing a career path, deciding where to live, or defining my parenting style, the clash was like mixing oil and water, both valuable but fundamentally different. It became a constant balancing act, trying to assert my individuality while respecting my family's values, and it often felt like walking on a tightrope suspended between two worlds.

The biggest challenge for me is cross-cultural communication. I prefer direct communication that is low context, but I've learned this can sometimes be seen as impolite by colleagues or acquaintances who value more indirect communication. At first, it was a bit stressful for me when working with colleagues from high-context cultures. They'd often use twenty to forty words to convey a message that could be said in just ten. As someone who values time and efficiency, this was a bit frustrating. I eventually understood this was just a cultural difference, not personal.

I've learned much about Dominican culture and its influence on my family's values. It's made me realize how different cultures can have different approaches to family, whether it's more focused on the group or the individual. Exploring the various elements that make up a culture, like language, religion, power dynamics, gender roles, communication styles, societal norms, and political systems, helps me put everything in context and understand how it fits into my own life. This has also helped me understand and appreciate other cultures better.

Exploring my culture, I discovered how traditions encompass more than language, holidays, festivals, and food. As the cultural iceberg highlights, they also involve beliefs, values, biases, and other less visible attributes. It's essential to comprehend these profound aspects of culture to understand one's own and other cultures better.

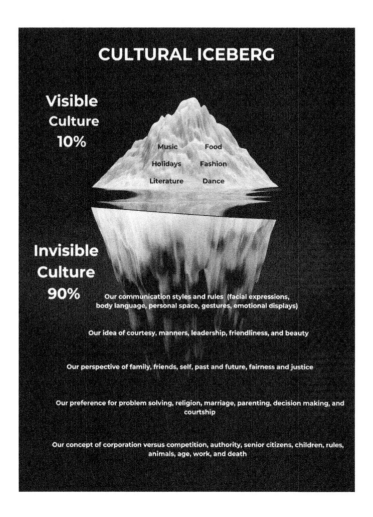

The cultural iceberg is like an intricate puzzle that reveals only its surface at first glance, tempting you to believe you've solved it. But dig deeper, and you discover hidden layers that complete the picture, each piece representing different aspects like norms, beliefs, and values. Cultural intelligence is the skill of not just observing the surface but diving deep to understand what lies beneath, making it possible to comprehend and navigate diverse worlds truly.

Understanding how culture includes overt and covert elements is a powerful tool. Overt aspects, like language, attire, festivities, and cuisine, can be easily recognized. However, covert elements, such as prejudices, cultural principles, family, and the justice system, are more subjective and implied. The iceberg symbolizes both macro and micro aspects of culture, allowing us to understand how these visible and invisible cultural attributes impact individuals' behavior, thoughts, and actions within a particular culture. On a macro level, it reveals various attributes combined to create a complete cultural identity.

CQ proved to be an invaluable resource in broadening my perspective on cultural diversity. Through its insights, I have come to realize that cultural norms are not only diverse within countries, but they also transcend ethnicity. Additionally, I now understand it is crucial to consider these differences when navigating different regions of the world and within the same country.

Follow me as we explore how the **C.H.O.I.C.E.** playbook helps us use our knowledge to understand ourselves and others.

PERSPECTIVE

Taking perspective is vital in grasping both the overt and covert elements of culture, as it deepens our understanding of the visible practices and the underlying values that shape us.

Understand your heritage: How might understanding your heritage deepen your ability to empathize and connect with individuals from different backgrounds?

Expand your perspective: If you discovered unexpected elements in your ancestry, how would that broaden your perspective on cultural diversity and complexity?

Trace your family history: How can tracing your family's migration story enhance your understanding of global cultural dynamics and their impact on individual lives?

Understand family traditions: Would uncovering your ancestral culture's traditions, values, and social norms equip you with a more nuanced approach to navigating cultural differences?

Lean into your unique identity: How could your personal experiences, culture, and identity, influenced by your heritage, serve as a lens for interpreting and appreciating the diverse experiences of others?

CHAPTER 11

C.H.O.I.C.E. Playbook

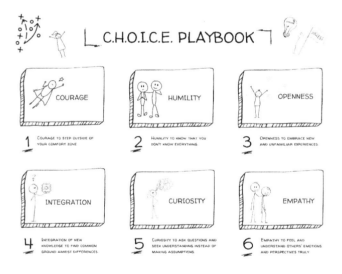

The world is more connected than ever, making Cultural Intelligence (CQ) and Cultural Humility essential. This playbook offers a comprehensive approach to developing these skills, emphasizing courage, humility, openness, integration, curiosity, and empathy.

Cultural Intelligence (CQ): Consider it a "social compass" that helps you navigate and connect with people worldwide and those in your neighborhood. As different countries have unique ways, so do the diverse groups in our local communities. Imagine you're a cultural detective. CQ equips you with the tools to read a room, understand the cultural norms, and act accordingly.

CQ helps you understand and relate to everyone, near or far. The CQ framework includes four capabilities: CQ Knowledge, CQ Strategy, CQ Drive, and CQ Action, with eleven subdimensions in total (Van Dyne et al. 2012, 298).

- **CQ Knowledge**: It's like your cultural "library." Think of it as your "cultural encyclopedia" in your brain. It's what you know about different cultures, including their customs, values, and norms.

- **CQ Strategy**: It's your game plan. It's how you plan to approach and navigate multicultural interactions and reflect on those plans afterward.

- **CQ Drive**: This inner battery drives you to be culturally aware. It's your motivation or drive to adapt and be effective in diverse settings.

- **CQ Action**: It's "walking the talk." This is how you put your strategy into action to adapt and perform in a diverse situation, like modifying your speech or actions based on the cultural context.

Cultural Humility: It is all about stepping back and really listening to what others say makes them, well, them. It's not just about what you think you know about their culture. It's about what they actually feel and believe (Tervalon and Murray-García 1998, 120). Unlike other cultural training methods that might give you a checklist of "dos and don'ts" for dealing with different groups, cultural humility is recognizing you don't have all the answers. It's about keeping an open mind and respecting how others define their heritage and identity (Hook et al. 2013, 1).

C.H.O.I.C.E.

The **C.H.O.I.C.E.** model invites people to have the *Courage* to step out of their comfort zones; the *Humility* to acknowledge that other perspectives exist while committing to lifelong self-reflection and learning; the *Openness* to embrace new and unfamiliar experiences; the *Integration* of new knowledge to find common ground amidst differences; the *Curiosity* to ask questions and seek understanding instead of making assumptions; and the *Empathy* to feel and understand others' emotions and perspectives truly.

Activating the **C.H.O.I.C.E.** model helps people create authentic relationships and cultivate a life rich with intention, multicultural understanding, and connection. You're living in a world buzzing with cultural diversity, whether you're navigating global business or just the local supermarket. Understanding how to interact effectively with people from different backgrounds isn't just a "nice-to-have." It's essential.

This playbook will guide you in applying the principles of Cultural Intelligence (CQ) and Cultural Humility to make you a more effective, appreciative, and harmonious human being in everyday life. Culture isn't just about countries. It's about the community group, the social club, your workplace, and even your family. Living with Cultural Intelligence (CQ) is about respectfully understanding and navigating these diverse ecosystems.

WHY C.H.O.I.C.E.?

In a world as interconnected as ours, the ability to communicate and connect across diverse backgrounds is more than a soft skill. It's a life skill. Here's your guide to infusing your daily life with CQ, using a dash of Cultural Humility, and embodying the spirit of **C.H.O.I.C.E.** that sets you up for personal and professional success.

ROADMAP

PART 1—CHANGE MANAGEMENT

Components: *CQ Strategy, CQ Knowledge, Cultural Humility, Change Management*

Goal: To lead and adapt through change, leveraging your cultural intelligence and humility.

Activities:

1. Plan: Identify the change you are making in your personal or professional life.

2. Stakeholder mapping: Identify how this change impacts personal and professional relationships.

3. Communication strategy: Create an inclusive communication plan, considering cultural factors, and share it with your personal and professional stakeholders.

Reflection: How do your CQ and cultural humility influence your change management approach?

PART 2: UNDERSTANDING YOUR IDENTITY

Components: *CQ Knowledge, CQ Strategy, Cultural Humility*

Goal: To recognize and understand the layers of your cultural, social, and personal identity.

Activities:

1. Self-audit: List your affiliations—ethnicity, nationality, religious, professional, etc.

2. Identity map: Use a Venn diagram to show how these affiliations intersect.

3. Perspective: How do these affiliations shape your worldview, values, and actions?

Reflection: In what situations do you feel a particular part of your identity is most pronounced? Did one part of your identity influence the other? What changes when you blend them?

PART 3: DEEPEN CULTURAL KNOWLEDGE

Components: CQ Knowledge, CQ Strategy, Cultural Humility

Goal: To acquire fundamental knowledge about different cultures and social groups.

Activities:

1. Cultural deep dive: Research a culture's core values and customs different from yours from credible and unbiased sources.

2. Interviews: Have coffee with someone from that culture and learn from their lived experience.

3. Synthesize: Combine your research and interview insights to form your understanding.

Reflection: What assumptions did you have before, and how have they changed? How will you integrate what you learned into your own life?

PART 4: DEVELOP CULTURAL HUMILITY

Components: Cultural Humility, CQ Drive

Goal: To develop an attitude of openness and a willingness to engage in lifelong self-development and learning about cultural diversity.

Activities:

1. Awareness journal: Record moments you felt culturally uncomfortable and what you learned daily.

2. Active listening: In conversations, make it a habit to understand what you hear by repeating or paraphrasing the other person's point to confirm your understanding.

3. Solicit feedback: Ask people from diverse backgrounds for constructive feedback on your cultural interactions.

Reflection: Can you recall a situation where cultural humility helped or could have helped? How did the situation help you understand better? How does the feedback differ from your perspective?

PART 5: APPLY WHAT YOU LEARN

Components: *CQ Action, Cultural Humility*

Goal: To practice integrating what you learn throughout your journey.

Activities:

1. Apply one new learning each week.

2. Seek feedback from trusted sources about your progress.

3. Share one new learning with friends or colleagues.

Reflection: How does the feedback compare with your perspective on your progress? What surprises you?

PART 6: KAIZEN

Components: *CQ Strategy, CQ Action, CQ Drive, Cultural Humility*

Goal: To adopt a lifelong CQ, Cultural Humility practice.

Activities:

1. Quarterly review: Look back at your activities, reflections, and what you learned.

2. Mentorship: Seek mentorship and mentor others regarding the lessons you learned.

3. Stay updated: Read books and articles and attend webinars to keep your knowledge fresh.

Reflection: What are the next steps in your journey toward becoming culturally intelligent? What excites you the most about your journey?

TOOLS FOR PERSPECTIVE TAKING AND SEEKING

- Daily journaling: Keep a **C.H.O.I.C.E.** journal where you jot down interesting interactions or thoughts with diverse cultures.

- Role-reversal exercises: Put yourself in someone else's shoes during a conflict or misunderstanding to gain new perspectives.

- Community involvement: Volunteer at community centers that cater to diverse populations.

- Create a culture board with people who offer different perspectives. Use the board as a sounding board in your cultural journey.

CHECKLIST FOR WEEKLY REVIEW

- Did I initiate a cross-cultural conversation?

- Did I attend an event that broadened my perspectives?

- Did I try a new cultural experience?

- Have I integrated a new cultural norm into my life?

- Did I share a news story from a diverse cultural perspective?

- Did I engage with content that elevated my humility and empathy?

- Did I disrupt a longstanding bias?

Remember, cultural intelligence is a journey, not a destination. Feel free to iterate these exercises and make this playbook your own. Incorporating these actions and reflections into your everyday life helps cultivate an ethos grounded in cultural intelligence and humility. You'll not only understand the world better but also enrich the world's understanding of you. So go ahead, make the **C.H.O.I.C.E.** today!

CHAPTER 12

Courage

Everything can be taken from a man but one thing: the last of the human freedoms—to choose one's attitude in any given set of circumstances, to choose one's own way.

—VIKTOR FRANKL

SUMMONING COURAGE

Since I was introduced to the concept of Cultural Intelligence (CQ), I knew I had embarked on a transformational journey that shifted how I viewed and interacted with the world.

I used to be a stickler about time and schedules, but working with a global team taught me to be more flexible, tolerant, and understanding of time orientation differences. I also struggled to understand why some colleagues hesitated to speak up in front of superiors. CQ helped me understand that other cultures view hierarchy as a sign of respect and order. Reflecting on my beliefs about power dynamics led to more inclusive team discussions.

I value being straightforward, while some friends and colleagues value group harmony. But I've realized that silence or indirectness doesn't always mean avoiding the issue. It can also be a way of expressing disagreement or respecting authority. Confronting my biases head-on enhanced my active listening skills to help others feel like I valued and respected their perspective. The same word, phrase, or gesture could mean entirely different things in different cultures. I learned to summon the courage to ask questions and clarify my point, ensuring my message was understood as intended.

Building trust took center stage. Trust, I realized, is developed differently across cultures. While I valued results-oriented trust, many friends and colleagues leaned toward relationship-based trust. CQ gave me the understanding to summon the courage to step out of my comfort zone. I began investing time in building personal relationships, understanding that shared personal stories and experiences could be as bonding as shared work successes.

Looking back on my journey, I am grateful for the insights that CQ has offered me. CQ has expanded my worldview, enabling me to understand cultural nuances with empathy and understanding. It has been a journey of growth, connection, and continuous learning, which I am still proudly on.

EMILY

Throughout the series, Emily courageously navigates cultural challenges, aiding in her professional growth and personal journey of self-discovery in a new city (Fleming 2020).

She's used to a more punctual start to the workday in the US and is shocked when her Parisian colleagues stroll in late to work. Instead of getting frustrated, she adjusts to this relaxed time orientation, understanding it as part of the work-life balance in French culture (Fleming 2020).

Emily is accustomed to a more informal and collaborative approach with her boss in the US. Eventually, she learns to appreciate the hierarchical structure. Still, she also bravely presents her ideas directly to Sylvie, challenging the traditional power distance courteously in ways that Sylvie does not always welcome (Fleming 2020).

Emily doesn't shy away from conflicts, addressing them head-on. Instead of causing a roadblock, she tries to find a middle ground when she disagrees with designer Pierre

Cadault. Emily faces language and communication barriers but learns French and uses humor to build colleague relationships. Emily is focused on achieving success in her job, but she learns to appreciate the French emphasis on enjoying life, experiencing moments, and building relationships. She takes time to enjoy Paris, attending events or just relaxing at a café, understanding that "being" is as essential as "doing" (Fleming 2020).

Emily consistently builds trust with her Parisian colleagues by delivering on her promises, showing commitment to team success, and respecting French traditions and sentiments. She also attempts to make amends after a perfume campaign goes awry due to her misunderstanding of French sensibilities, solidifying trust (Fleming 2020).

SAM

For Sam, courage was not about grand gestures. Instead, it manifested in the small, daily decisions to communicate, adapt, and try to understand a worldview different from his own. Sam's commitment to punctuality made him hyper-aware of time's importance. When Clara changed meeting times or let sessions run over, it took courage for Sam to communicate his needs directly.

Initially, Sam found it odd when Clara sought his input on meetings. In his past experiences, managers didn't usually ask for feedback. Summing up the courage, Sam begins offering Clara suggestions when asked. This initiative shows Clara that Sam will bridge the gap and subtly shift their power dynamics to a more collaborative relationship. Sam bravely approaches Clara to discuss their differences and his need for structure and predictability. As a result, Clara adjusts her leadership style to accommodate him.

One of Sam's bravest steps is disclosing his Asperger's and explaining how it influences his work style. Sharing his personal information gives Clara the context to better understand his reactions and preferences.

Clara's emphasis on relationship-building seems extraneous to task-oriented Sam. Yet, he recognizes the value Clara places on "being" rather than just "doing." So, he courageously decides to step out of his comfort zone, scheduling brief one-on-one sessions. These controlled interactions allowed Sam to be present without getting overwhelmed.

Given their stark differences, trust is initially a significant challenge. Sam's courageous vulnerability about his needs and his attempts to understand Clara's perspective cultivate mutual trust. Sam's story underlines the beauty of diversity and the strength of collaboration when two individuals decide to meet halfway.

EUGINA

Eugina Jordan, author of *UNLIMITED: The Seventeen Proven Laws for Success in a Workplace Not Designed for You*, epitomizes courage. Not only did she write the book to encourage inclusion, but she also dedicated her life to empowering others to be unlimited. As a single mom and Russian immigrant, she learned to develop strategies to navigate the challenges that stem from cultural differences while leveraging the power of networking, catapulting her career growth toward the C-suite role she holds today. Despite the challenges she faces, she dedicates her life to uplifting others. She finds that courage helps her thrive despite the hurdles she faces.

"I embarked on a journey to rewire my communication habits, focusing on being upfront and direct while preserving respect. Over time, I shed the inclination to beat around the bush and embraced transparent discussions. As I evolved, my interactions with colleagues improved—they valued my newfound clarity and authenticity. This experience taught me that self-awareness and adaptability are crucial in navigating cross-cultural differences, and by honing my communication skills, I turned a challenge into an opportunity for growth," she said.

"As a Russian-born professional, my approach to resolving a conflict with an underperforming employee was deeply rooted in empathy. Understanding the significance of building strong connections, I recognized that a compassionate approach could potentially yield more positive outcomes," she explained.

CREATING MOMENTS THAT MATTER

Unraveling the threads of our cultural heritage and history can be a transformative journey, and understanding the impact on our cultural values can profoundly shape our interactions with the world. Here are five experiential activities to help you courageously embrace your cultural heritage, explore different perspectives, and develop a deeper self-awareness and cultural intelligence.

ACTIVITY 1: DISCOVERING YOUR ROOTS

Components: CQ Knowledge, CQ Drive

Goal: To explore your family history and cultural heritage to reignite curiosity about your roots.

Action plan:

- Research your family tree using online platforms or interviewing family elders.

- Record stories, traditional practices, or recipes.

Perspective-taking questions:

- What were the shared values and practices in your ancestors' time?

- How might these values have shaped your family's current practices and values?

ACTIVITY 2: CULTURAL ARTIFACT SHOW-AND-TELL

Components: CQ Action, Cultural Humility

Goal: To physically connect with your heritage and acknowledge and honor its significance.

Action plan:

- Find an artifact or heirloom representing your culture (e.g., jewelry or traditional clothing).

- Share its story with friends, explaining its significance and origin.

Perspective-taking questions:

- What emotions did you feel sharing your artifact's story?

- How did the listeners' perspectives or reactions enhance your understanding?

ACTIVITY 3: HERITAGE ROLE PLAY

Components: CQ Strategy, CQ Drive

Goal: To immerse yourself in an ancestor's role and understand the challenges they faced.

Action plan:

- Choose a historical period from your ancestry.

- Role-play a day in an ancestor's life with friends or family from that period.

Perspective-taking questions:

- How did the day-to-day challenges shape your ancestor's values?

- What cultural practices from that time persist today, and why?

ACTIVITY 4: MAPPING THE INTANGIBLES

Components: *CQ Knowledge, Cultural Humility*

Goal: To visually represent cultural values and develop a deeper appreciation for their origins.

Action plan:

- List down values you believe come from your cultural heritage.

- Create a visual map showing connections between values, historical events, or cultural practices.

Perspective-taking questions:

- How have certain events or practices influenced the values you hold dear today?

- Are there values you'd want to revive or understand more deeply?

ACTIVITY 5: CULTURAL LISTENING CIRCLES

Components: *CQ Action, CQ Strategy*

Goal: To cultivate openness and respect and challenge and refine your understanding.

Action plan:

- Create a safe space with friends from diverse backgrounds to share stories or experiences about your cultural values.

- Listen actively, then share your insights about your heritage.

Perspective-taking questions:

- How did others' cultural stories resonate with or differ from yours?

- What new insights did you gain about your cultural values and their origins?

Remember, the journey to understanding your cultural heritage is deeply personal yet universally relatable. As you dig deeper, keep an open heart and mind. No matter how small, every insight brings you closer to understanding yourself and your intricate heritage kaleidoscope.

CHAPTER 13

Humility

—

Pride is concerned with who is right. Humility is concerned with what is right.

—EZRA TAFT BENSON

HUMBLING MYSELF

Accepting the courage to confront my biases was a humbling experience. Deconstructing them became a powerful catalyst for change.

I always found myself at the intersection of many worlds.

This duality became more pronounced as I grew older. I also grappled with the complexities of my identity. Yet, my unique perspective often made me exceptionally attuned to the struggles of those who felt caught between cultures.

But my journey wasn't always smooth. With my upper-middle-class economic status, I sometimes straddled the line of privilege and the grounded reality I came from. The memories of my parents' struggles to provide for me juxtaposed with my now comfortable life often play on my mind.

When I confronted my biases, I learned to understand the intricate interplay of my identity and societal factors. My cultural background, while diverse, was just a part of my identity. I'm not just a neurodivergent Afro-Latina, Gen-Xer, or daughter of Dominican immigrants. I am a sum of all these parts and learned to appreciate each identity with pride.

I see all aspects of my cultural identity as a rich tapestry woven from various threads, each representing a facet of my life. I am multidimensional, and so is everyone else.

I draw from this tapestry daily, using my unique experiences and perspectives to understand, empathize, and guide others.

In my heart, I carry the rhythms of merengue and bachata (traditional Dominican dances), the grit of neurodivergence, the revolutionary spirit of a Gen-Xer, the determination and ambition of my immigrant parents, and the privileges and responsibilities of my economic status.

Connecting with my heritage helped link aspects of my identity that forged a deeper understanding of the cultural differences around me.

EMILY

Emily's journey from a confident, sometimes overzealous executive to a more culturally sensitive individual showcases the importance of understanding, adaptability, and humility in our diverse world (Fleming 2020).

In her early days, Emily believes her American business ways seamlessly translate into the French work environment. She's quickly met with resistance, confusion, and even ridicule. As Emily navigates her professional and personal life, she faces numerous challenges, from misinterpreting casual kisses on the cheeks to mishandling delicate situations at work due to her direct approach. These experiences serve as mirrors, reflecting her cultural biases and misconceptions. Slowly, she realizes her way isn't the only way, nor is it always the right way in a different cultural setting (Fleming 2020).

Recognizing her gaps, Emily turns to her new friends and colleagues for guidance. Mindy, her vivacious friend, often serves as a cultural interpreter, helping Emily decode French social norms. Through these interactions, Emily doesn't just learn about French culture. She learns about how they intersect with humility. She begins to ask more questions, observe more keenly, and listen more actively (Fleming 2020).

One of Emily's strengths is her adaptability. Her journey is punctuated with mistakes but becomes humbler with each misstep. Instead of being defensive, she becomes more receptive to feedback. This humility doesn't translate to losing her identity but is about acknowledging, respecting, and valuing differences to coexist (Fleming 2020).

JAKE

Jake's journey in cultural intelligence is a testament to the power of humility in leadership. One of the first indicators of Jake's humility comes when he realizes the limitations of his individualistic approach. His team, primarily from collectivist cultures, values group cohesion over personal achievement. Jake does not hold onto his values rigidly when presented with this insight. Instead, he integrates more collaborative strategies, recognizing that the team's diverse viewpoints could lead to innovative solutions.

Jake's humility also shines through in how he deals with communication styles. Jake is from a low-context culture where straightforwardness is the norm. When his high-context colleagues find this overwhelming and confront him, Jake listens. Instead of dismissing their feedback, he appreciates their effort to step out of their comfort zone for clarity and validates their opinion. This acknowledgment is a powerful testament to his humility and willingness to learn and adapt, even when the lessons come from unexpected places.

Jake's humility is also evident in his approach to risk-taking. His low uncertainty avoidance makes him comfortable with ambiguity, but some of his team members prefer a more cautious approach. Jake doesn't override them or discount their contributions when they express this. Instead, he takes the time to understand the merits of a more structured risk analysis, highlighting his ability to humble himself to value other perspectives.

Jake acknowledges how his team educates him, encapsulating his entire approach: a willingness to admit what he doesn't know and an openness to learn, even when in a leadership position.

Embracing humility doesn't just make Jake improve as a leader. He elevates his entire team. He understands that managing cultural diversity is a collective effort, and humility doesn't weaken his leadership, it enhances it, providing a rich soil where the seeds of mutual respect and understanding can grow. This approach transforms his team's challenges into their greatest strengths, setting the stage for unparalleled success.

MIRNA

Mirna is the essence of humility. As a Latina immigrant who identifies as a female working in a male-dominated industry, Mirna faced insurmountable challenges that would have otherwise prevented her from succeeding. Between her heavy accent, gender role, and immigrant status, she faced insurmountable challenges at work. What separates Mirna from the rest is that she returned to school to obtain a degree in cybersecurity when she already had one from her home country.

"I wanted to learn the language in a way that I could speak the technical language at work," she told me. "The experience helped me understand the technical language and humbled me in ways that help me pave the way for others."

CREATING MOMENTS THAT MATTER

Cultivating humility is a cornerstone of Cultural Intelligence (CQ) and Cultural Humility. Here are five activities that help build humility by better understanding different cultures and perspectives.

ACTIVITY 1: CULTURAL EXCHANGE DAY

Components: *CQ Action, CQ Knowledge, Cultural Humility*

Goal: Practice adaptability and understanding cultural norms to enhance cultural awareness and humility.

Action plan:

- Pair up with someone from a different cultural background.

- Spend a day together, each taking turns introducing each other to a cultural activity, food, or custom.

- Reflect on the experience.

Perspective-taking questions:

- What new norms did you notice, and how did you adapt your behavior?

- Did anything surprise you or challenge your previous beliefs?

ACTIVITY 2: LOCAL CULTURAL EXPLORATION

CQ components: CQ Strategy, CQ Drive

Goal: Increase motivation to explore cultural differences to improve strategic thinking about cultural interactions.

Action plan:

- Choose a local cultural event or location you've never visited before.

- Attend the event or visit the location and observe.

- Create a strategy for engaging meaningfully with this culture in the future.

Perspective-taking and seeking questions:

- How did you feel going into this new experience?

- How would you prepare differently next time?

ACTIVITY 3: THE "WHY" BEHIND THE "WHAT" JOURNAL

Components: *CQ Knowledge, Cultural Humility*

Goal: Develop a deep understanding of your cultural background to build cultural humility through self-reflection.

Action plan:

- Maintain a journal documenting your daily activities and cultural interactions.

- Next to each entry, note why you think you act the way you do, linking it to your cultural values or norms.

Perspective-taking questions:

- What aspects of your own culture have you perhaps taken for granted?

- How can understanding the "why" behind your actions help you understand the actions of others?

ACTIVITY 4: CULTURAL NORM NEGOTIATION ROLE-PLAY

Components: *CQ Action, CQ Strategy, CQ Knowledge*

Goal: To practice adaptability in real-world, complex scenarios and develop strategic planning skills for multicultural situations.

Action plan:

- With a group of friends or colleagues, set up a role-play exercise involving negotiation between two cultures.

- Swap roles to experience both sides.

Perspective-taking questions:

- What did you find challenging in adapting to the different negotiation styles?

- How would you change your strategy for next time?

ACTIVITY 5: SELF-ASSESSMENT AND PEER FEEDBACK

Components: *CQ Drive, Cultural Humility*

Goal: Strengthen intrinsic motivation for cultural learning and cultivate an attitude of lifelong learning and openness.

Action plan:

- Take an online CQ self-assessment.

- Share your results with a trusted friend and ask for candid feedback on areas you could improve.

Perspective-taking questions:

- What is driving your interest in improving your CQ?

- How open are you to receiving and acting upon feedback to become more culturally humble?

These activities help you immerse yourself in the ongoing cultural understanding and humility journey. The true richness lies in the continuous exploration, learning, and adaptability that come with it. So, dive in, reflect, adapt, and enjoy the journey! They can be a starting point for long-term growth and continuous learning.

CHAPTER 14

Openness

Just try new things. Don't be afraid. Step out of your comfort zones and soar, all right?
—MICHELLE OBAMA

"I've never eaten Indian food," I explained to a friend.

"Never?" she asked.

"No, never," I said.

I was explaining to a friend that I was excited to eat Indian food at an upcoming wedding I was attending. Until then, I had no interest in trying Indian food. After attending the wedding, I became an Indian food enthusiast and searched for Indian restaurants in my neighborhood. The experience awakened my senses in ways unimagined.

EMILY

In the heart of Paris, Emily Cooper's life was blossoming in ways she hadn't imagined. Fresh from the US, she was thrown into a whirlwind of French elegance, confusion, and chaos, and her cultural intelligence journey had just begun (Fleming 2020).

While dining at a French restaurant, Emily finds her steak undercooked and complains to the waiter. Despite her insistence, the waiter defends the chef's preparation. Emily's friend, Mindy, jestingly mentions the classic belief in France that customers aren't always right. Emily's frustration peaks, prompting her to challenge the chef's knowledge of customer service (Fleming 2020).

But Mindy humorously points out the audacity of trying to alter a deeply rooted French culinary tradition over a steak. Undeterred, Emily considers giving the chef, Gabriel, a lesson in customer service. To her surprise, Gabriel appears at their table to address the issue. Emily quickly changes her tune, claiming everything is perfect. Skeptically, Gabriel urges her to try the steak before he takes it back. Tentatively, Emily takes a bite and discovers the steak is delicious, just as Gabriel had confidently predicted (Fleming 2020).

Emily's openness to new experiences, albeit forced sometimes, is evident throughout her new life in Paris. She approaches it with curiosity, learning, and adapting, yet staying true to her feelings and values. She makes blunders and laughs at herself, but most importantly, she learns. Paris isn't just a city of love for Emily but of learning, growth, and endless adventures. And as the Seine River shimmers under the Parisian sun, Emily's journey of cultural exploration flows seamlessly, enriching her life in myriad ways (Fleming 2020).

SOFIE

In New York City, Sofie absorbs the city's nuances. Skyscrapers loom tall, casting shadows on the streets below, and people rush by her, each engrossed in their world. It's an overwhelming symphony of sights, sounds, and energy, but Sofie embraces it.

Every morning, Sofie navigates the subway maze while conversing with fellow commuters. Although New Yorkers are not known for subway small talk, Sofie's French-accented English and genuine interest in their stories soon encourage sharing anecdotes and offering recommendations.

Her colleagues at work are in awe of her curiosity. During lunch breaks, she sits with a different group daily, laughing and learning about New York's best-kept secrets. Her curiosity isn't just casual. She takes notes, planning to explore each suggested spot.

On weekends, Sofie is always out and about. On Saturday, she enjoys spicy street food at a food festival in Queens, her face showing a mix of surprise and delight with every bite. The following weekend, she visits a jazz bar in Harlem, moving along to the beat and becoming fully immersed in the music and the crowd.

Her apartment is a mix of old and new. French cookbooks sit alongside books from a local bakery specializing in fusion French-American pastries. The scents of her cooking experiments waft through the hallways, drawing neighbors to her door. Sofie greets them with infectious enthusiasm and insists they try a bite and give feedback.

One day, a colleague invites Sofie to a high-intensity spin class—a far cry from her usual countryside cycling. Sofie accepts and emerges exhilarated, a testament to her willingness to step out of her comfort zone.

She attends a local library's discussion group in the evenings, where she stands out with her animated demeanor and thought-provoking questions. Her genuine interest and unique expatriate perspective draw people toward her during breaks.

Sofie immerses herself in every New York adventure, celebrating differences.

RIHAB

After living in twenty countries, Rihab's life experiences embody openness. Although she enjoys the excitement of living in a new place, she is now settled in Boston with her family.

"Living in so many places can be a blessing and a curse," she admitted.

I met Rihab while collaborating with a group for International Women in Business. When she shares her experiences, she does so with genuine curiosity about the world around her.

"My experiences humbled me," she said. "Although I have emotional intelligence, cultural intelligence enhanced my EQ and humbled me further."

CREATING MOMENTS THAT MATTER

These activities are designed to get you involved and consider different cultures actively. They'll challenge you to step out of your comfort zone and remind you to respect other people's traditions and beliefs. Thinking deeply about these experiences is essential. It helps you understand how they shape the way you see and interact with the world.

ACTIVITY 1: "YES, AND..." WEEK

Components: *CQ Action, CQ Drive*

Goal: To boost adaptability and increase motivation for new experiences.

Action plan:

- For one week, say "Yes, and..." to opportunities that arise, especially those you'd usually shy away from.

- Keep a diary to record these experiences.

Perspective-taking questions:

- How did saying yes impact your mood and openness?

- Were there moments when saying yes was difficult? Why?

ACTIVITY 2: THE CULTURAL NEWS SWAP

Components: *CQ Knowledge, CQ Strategy*

Goal: To understand global current events and expand your views on global issues.

Action plan:

- Partner up with a friend and assign each other a different country.

- Both of you find a news article from your respective countries and swap.

- Discuss how the news impacts your understanding of that culture and global affairs.

Perspective-taking questions:

- What surprised you about the article you read?

- How could you strategize to engage with people from this culture in the future?

ACTIVITY 3: THE EMPATHY WALK

Components: CQ Action, Cultural Humility

Goal: To practice active listening and develop humility through understanding others.

Action plan:

- Take a thirty-minute walk with a friend or family member.

- Spend fifteen minutes where one person talks and the other only listens, then switch.

Perspective-taking questions:

- How did it feel just to listen? What did you observe?

- Did this activity change the way you perceive the other person?

ACTIVITY 4: VIRTUAL CULTURAL IMMERSION

Components: *CQ Knowledge, CQ Strategy*

Goal: To gain knowledge of a new culture and plan how you would interact within this culture.

Action plan:

- Choose a culture you know little about.

- Watch a documentary or read extensively about it.

- Strategize how you'd navigate a typical day in that culture.

Perspective-taking questions:

- What new social norms did you learn?

- How would you navigate a day in this culture based on your learning?

ACTIVITY 5: LEFT/RIGHT HAND REVERSAL DAY

Components: *CQ Drive, Cultural Humility*

Goal: To challenge personal norms and habits and cultivate self-awareness and humility.

Action plan:

- Choose a day to switch your dominant hand. If you're right-handed, try using your left hand or vice versa for simple tasks.

- Journal the experience, focusing on how it felt to alter familiar habits.

Perspective-taking questions:

- What did you find difficult, and why?

- How has this experience made you consider the challenges others face when adapting to new cultural norms?

Completing these activities facilitates new experiences. Remember, the journey toward greater cultural intelligence and openness is ongoing. Ask questions, step out of your comfort zone, and embrace life's extraordinary diversity.

CHAPTER 15

Integration

*Tell me and I forget, teach me and I may remember, involve
me and I learn.*
—BENJAMIN FRANKLIN

I have copious notes about many topics. Sometimes, they
might transform into "Loren'sms," which are more personal

and intimate communications, or evolve into research materials for my professional or academic endeavors. These notes often form the basis of my insightful observations shared on various social media platforms. What I love the most about this practice is that sharing these notes and insights with others significantly helps me retain and integrate what I learn. Embracing this method enriches my learning experience and allows me to contribute to the collective knowledge within my community.

EMILY

Emily Cooper, our fearless protagonist in *Emily in Paris*, is not your typical American-in-Paris caricature. Sure, she lands in the City of Light armed with a high-school-level grasp of the French language and an unquenchable thirst for adventure, but she's also a sponge for cultural nuance. And trust me, Paris gives her plenty to soak up (Fleming 2020)

First, let's chat about her work life. Emily dives headfirst into Savoir, the marketing firm she's sent to "Americanize." But she quickly learns it's not just about speaking French. It's about speaking "French workplace." For example, once, she tries to schedule a lunch meeting, and everyone looks at her as if she's suggested eating snails for breakfast. Lunch in Paris is sacred—no business talk allowed. And instead of insisting on her American ways, she adapts. By the next episode, Emily is savoring leisurely Parisian lunches, no iPhone in sight, and yes, sometimes there's wine involved. She learns to do business the French way—with nuanced understanding, long discussions, and an air of diplomacy as smooth as the local Bordeaux (Fleming 2020).

But Emily doesn't stop at the office. She knows culture is absorbed better with people than with books. Enter Mindy, the Chinese expat who becomes her go-to confidant in the city. Through their friendship, Emily explores another layer of Paris—where expats from all corners of the world converge. She takes it all in, showing us that cultural nuance isn't just about blending in. It's about understanding the various threads that make up the social fabric (Fleming 2020).

Ah, love. We can't talk about Emily without diving into her romantic escapades. Boy, does she have her plate full! Gabriel, her hunky neighbor and chef, is boyfriend material, but he has a girlfriend, Camille. Emily could easily step on some toes in an environment laden with hidden rules and unwritten codes. But she navigates this tricky territory with impressive awareness. She respects Camille, understanding the French perspective on love and relationships is more fluid but equally deep. It's not just about "hook-up culture" or "finding the one." It's an intricate dance, and Emily learns the steps quickly, even if she stumbles occasionally (Fleming 2020).

And let's not forget fashion. Paris is the world's fashion capital, and Emily knows she has much to learn. She doesn't unthinkingly copy. Instead, she integrates. Her bold American styles merge effortlessly with Parisian elegance, resulting in an ensemble as unique as her personality. This isn't just about clothes. It's about identity. Emily shows us that integrating cultural nuances doesn't mean losing yourself but enriching who you already are (Fleming 2020).

SARAH

Sarah's journey of self-improvement begins with a deep-seated curiosity and an open mind. Tired of feeling like she's missing out on richer experiences, she takes a holistic approach to growth, blending principles of CQ and other interdisciplinary learnings into her daily life. The transformation is neither instantaneous nor easy, but it is gratifying.

She doesn't just hit the books or binge-watch documentaries to activate CQ Knowledge and understand why people from different cultures do what they do. She gets out there—talking to people, attending community events, and listening—to get the complete picture behind each culture.

To activate the CQ Strategy, Sarah regularly reflects on her interactions and experiences. She examines her assumptions, analyzes her successes and failures in intercultural interactions, and sets specific goals for the future. She notices her understanding of "personal space," for example, is very Western-centric. In some cultures, closer physical proximity is more common and not considered invasive. Recognizing this allows her to feel more comfortable in diverse settings.

A growing sense of enthusiasm fuels Sarah's CQ Drive. The more she learns, the more she wants to know. She ventures into cultural experiences that she might have previously avoided, bolstered by newfound courage and curiosity.

Whether it's trying exotic foods or engaging in conversations that she initially finds challenging, she pushes herself out of her comfort zone.

The most actionable change comes from CQ Action. She practices adaptability and problem-solving in real time. She no longer reacts impulsively to unfamiliar behaviors or traditions. Instead, she seeks to understand the context and adapt her behavior accordingly. From modifying her communication style to being mindful of hierarchical dynamics in professional settings, Sarah has become adept at reading the room—any room filled with people from any corner of the world.

Sarah finds that her Cultural Humility naturally deepens through this process. She understands that learning about other cultures doesn't make her an expert but a respectful and engaged global citizen. She is listening more than speaking, asking questions instead of assuming, and always, always willing to say, "I don't know. Could you help me understand?"

So, how does Sarah integrate all these lessons into her day-to-day life? It becomes a part of her. Her openness to new experiences is no longer forced. It comes naturally. Her work environment became a hub of inclusivity, her social circle expanded in diversity, and her family benefited from her enriched worldview. She cultivates empathy, easily stepping into others' shoes to walk and feel the ground they walk on. Above all, she finds that her world expands exponentially—all because she consciously chooses to grow, learn, and be more.

ENRIQUE

Enrique started his career as an electrical engineer, but after transferring to the United States for university, he discovered a passion for human resources. Leveraging the cultural intelligence he gained from his global experiences in and out of work, he made a career switch that felt right.

"I just fell in love with human resources and what it represents in an organization," he explains.

In HR, Enrique combines his technical expertise with his knack for understanding people from various backgrounds. Today, Enrique founded Hacking HR, a global learning community for everyone who plays a role in human resources, from the CEO to the practitioner. Enrique proves the most unconventional career paths can sometimes lead to fulfilling roles when you infuse cultural intelligence.

CREATING MOMENTS THAT MATTER

Making cultural intelligence and cultural humility a lived experience, not just a theoretical concept, is essential. Below are five hands-on activities that zero in on CQ Action, integrating other CQ components and Cultural Humility. These activities are designed to encourage you to incorporate cultural intelligence into your everyday life, with a focus on perspective-taking.

ACTIVITY 1: "WALK IN MY SHOES" ACTIVITY

Components: *CQ Action, CQ Drive*

Goal: Develop empathy and broaden your cultural outlook to engage empathetically with someone from a different cultural background.

Action plan:

- Identify a friend, colleague, or acquaintance from a different cultural background.

- Spend a day shadowing each other, sharing and discussing cultural experiences.

Perspective-taking questions:

- What did you find most surprising about their daily rituals or behaviors?

- What preconceived notions were challenged?

ACTIVITY 2: "CHOPPED" CULTURAL EDITION

Components: *CQ Action, CQ Knowledge*

Goal: Understand cultural significance through food and appreciate different cuisines and their cultural significance.

Action plan:

- Pick a foreign cuisine you are unfamiliar with. Research its cultural history.

- Attempt to cook a dish from that cuisine and invite friends to share the experience.

Perspective-taking questions:

- How did the ingredients and cooking techniques challenge your culinary norms?

- What have you learned about the culture through its food?

ACTIVITY 3: FILM CLUB FOR CULTURAL AWARENESS

Components: *CQ Action, CQ Strategy*

Goal: Enhance cultural understanding through cinema and build a nuanced understanding of different cultures through their storytelling.

Action plan:

- Once a month, watch a movie from a different country or featuring a different culture.

- Discuss the film with friends or family, focusing on cultural aspects.

Perspective-taking questions:

- What aspects of the culture were new to you?

- How did the film challenge or confirm your views on the represented culture?

ACTIVITY 4: THE "ROLE REVERSAL" EXERCISE

Components: *CQ Action, Cultural Humility*

Goal: To switch roles to understand power dynamics and cultural norms better.

Action plan:

- Choose a setting where you are usually in a role of cultural familiarity (e.g., hosting a dinner or leading a meeting).

- Switch roles with someone from a different culture, letting them lead while you follow.

Perspective-taking questions:

- How did it feel to relinquish control or familiarity?

- What did you learn from observing another's approach?

ACTIVITY 5: "CULTURE SHOCK" TRAVEL DAY

Components: *CQ Action, CQ Drive*

Goal: Experience "culture shock" without traveling abroad to expand your comfort zone and develop adaptability skills.

Action plan:

- Identify a cultural or ethnic neighborhood in your city you're unfamiliar with.

- Spend the day exploring, shopping, or dining in this area.

Perspective-taking questions:

- How did you navigate the unfamiliar setting?

- Were there moments you felt uncomfortable, and why?

With these activities, your objective is to "know" and "do"—to enact cultural intelligence practically and meaningfully. These exercises should help you integrate cultural understanding into your daily actions, nurturing your CQ and Cultural Humility.

CHAPTER 16

Curiosity

———

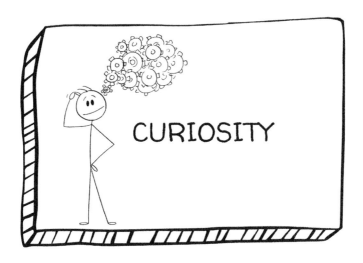

The important thing is not to stop questioning. Curiosity has its own reasons for existing.

—*ALBERT EINSTEIN*

CALL ME DORA!

My husband calls me "Dora the Explorer." Like *Dora the Explorer*, I approach every day as a new adventure waiting to unfold. Whether it's diving into an intriguing book, wandering through different neighborhoods, or engaging in enriching conversations, I'm always on a quest to learn something new and turn it into Loren'sms. This relentless curiosity doesn't just open doors. It builds bridges to new worlds and perspectives. Life is more than a series of events. It's a constant learning journey. I'm always asking questions to find answers and understand the layers of complexity that make up the world around me. Every day offers a new opportunity for discovery, and I'm eager to seize it. No matter where we go, I always look for lessons.

EMILY

The effervescent protagonist of *Emily in Paris* is the epitome of curiosity in action. From the moment she steps off the plane, wide-eyed and bundled in her chic wardrobe, she's like a sponge, ready to soak up everything the City of Light offers. But let's be honest, her curiosity isn't just about enjoying croissants and snapping Instagram-worthy pics of the Eiffel Tower. It's far more layered than that (Fleming 2020).

For starters, Emily displays professional curiosity. As a marketing exec sent to Paris to bring an American perspective to her French firm, she could easily coast by on her existing knowledge. But no, Emily doesn't settle. She takes it upon herself to understand the intricate nuances of French consumer culture. Whether she's brainstorming ways to promote a mattress, navigating social media trends, or pushing the boundaries with a perfume campaign, she's keen to get into the French mindset. Sometimes, she nails it, and other times, she flops, but the key is that she's always learning (Fleming 2020).

Then, there's cultural curiosity. Emily may stumble through awkward French phrases and misconstrue social cues—remember the awkward "la bise" (cheek kiss) moment?—but she never stops trying. Even when her landlady, Sylvie, or her coworker, Luc, throws cultural curveballs her way, Emily tries to figure things out. Her positive attitude fuels her curiosity as she embarks on new experiences, even if they're outside her comfort zone (Fleming 2020).

But don't let the "young woman in a big city" trope fool you. Emily's curiosity isn't just about her. It's also relational. She's intrigued by the people around her. She wants to know what makes her hunky neighbor Gabriel tick and what's happening with her boss Sylvie's icy demeanor. She doesn't just see people as stepping stones or problems. She sees them as puzzles, as stories waiting to unfold. This makes her a great friend, a thoughtful lover, and an empathetic coworker. She knows everyone has something to teach her, and she's all ears (Fleming 2020).

Emily has her cringe moments—we all do when we're stepping into a new world. But her unwavering curiosity elevates her from being just another expat in Paris to someone deeply engaged with her new home on multiple levels. And this is what makes her not just relatable but also inspiring. In a world where it's easy to stay in our little bubbles, Emily bursts through, reminding us of the richness of asking questions, seeking to understand, and being open to the unfamiliar. It's a lesson in how curiosity isn't just a trait. It's a lifestyle (Fleming 2020).

JACK

Remember Jack? He finds himself in a situation many in his generation can relate to in reporting to a significantly younger boss, representing different cultural and managerial values. From the outset, Jack recognizes a palpable difference in how he and Lisa approach work. Lisa, his millennial manager, champions an open, collaborative work environment emphasizing horizontal relationships over traditional hierarchies. While many might resist such a shift, Jack stands out for his curiosity in navigating this generational divide.

However, instead of dismissing Lisa's approach as inexperienced or counterproductive, Jack's curiosity nudges him to explore the reasoning behind their different perspectives.

Jack's curiosity is sparked by the unique intersectionality between his generational experience and his career in technology. Growing up during a significant technological change, he has a deeply rooted understanding of the evolution of innovation. Yet, he's equally fascinated by how the younger generation, the future torchbearers of technology, perceive and contribute to advancements in the field. This blend of generational insight and professional expertise doesn't just inform his work. It fuels an insatiable curiosity to explore what's next, bridging the gap between past experiences and future possibilities.

"I was curious about the new approaches and ideas that millennials like Lisa were contributing to technology," Jack said.

It's not just the jargon that intrigues him. It's the entirely different worldview Lisa and her generation seem to have regarding work, technology, and even success itself. He starts by asking Lisa for reading recommendations, wanting to understand the principles that shaped her management style. Lisa, pleasantly surprised by Jack's open-mindedness, shares a couple of articles and podcasts focusing on tech trends and modern workplace dynamics. Jack dives into them, trying to grasp the words and cultural ethos behind them.

But Jack doesn't stop at just intellectual curiosity. He takes it a step further. Realizing that new technological approaches often reflect deeper cultural shifts, he approached Lisa to discuss how the team could integrate these new ideas into their projects. Jack's questions are sincere and probing. "How can we apply a 'zero trust architecture' framework in our current project? How can it be a sustainable model for our team?" he asked Lisa.

Lisa engages in deep conversations with Jack about the future of work, conversations she hadn't expected to have with someone from a different generation. She appreciates his genuine questions and willingness to adapt and learn. For Jack, it opens a new avenue of understanding, not just about technology but also about the evolving cultural landscape that shapes these changes.

Jack's curiosity doesn't just bridge a generational gap. It also cultivates a more collaborative work environment. His team, including Lisa, admires his willingness to leave his comfort zone. By being curious, Jack demonstrates that adapting to new cultural norms and technological changes isn't just for the young. It is a choice available to anyone open enough to explore it.

"I am comfortable with my style, but I know I need to evolve like technology," admitted Jack.

GARY

When I met Gary at a conference a year ago, I knew I wanted to learn more from him. I was not only intrigued by his Irish accent but by his curiosity. Every question he asked was oozing with curiosity like sprinkles on ice cream. Gary, an Irish immigrant who moved to Ohio for university, embodies the power of curiosity and a growth mindset. Despite the culture shock and initial challenges of adapting to American life, Gary's positive attitude and inquisitive nature turned obstacles into opportunities for learning.

"I knew things were different and was curious to learn more," he tells me.

Instead of feeling overwhelmed, he immersed himself in local customs and formed genuine connections with people from various backgrounds. His curiosity not only enriched his own life but also positively influenced those around him. I can talk to Gary about anything, although I may be slightly biased since I am "Dora the Explorer." Through his journey, Gary shows that curiosity and a positive attitude can be the best tools for thriving in a new environment.

CREATING MOMENTS THAT MATTER

Curiosity is like a muscle—the more you use it, the stronger it becomes. It's like openness on steroids! Here are five activities designed to help you cultivate curiosity and integrate cultural knowledge seamlessly into your daily life. Each includes components of CQ Action, CQ Knowledge, CQ Strategy, and CQ Drive, as well as principles of cultural humility.

ACTIVITY 1: "FLAG" YOU'RE IT!

Components: *CQ Action, CQ Knowledge, Cultural Humility*

Goal: To expand your perspective and discover the history behind a country's flag.

Action plan:

- Select a country flag at random.

- Research the history behind the flag and what the different attributes represent.

- Discuss what you learned about the flag with a trusted friend or colleague.

Perspective-taking questions:

- What did you learn?

- How did your friend or colleague react when you shared what you learned?

ACTIVITY 2: WHY FOR A DAY

Components: *CQ Action, CQ Knowledge, CQ Drive*

Goal: To encourage curiosity, deepen understanding, and cultivate empathy by actively engaging with the world through a series of "why" questions.

Action plan:

- Spend a day asking "Why?" in conversations.

- When speaking with friends, family, or colleagues, pose a "why" question related to the topic of discussion.

Perspective-taking questions:

- What did you learn?

- How did people react when you asked why continuously?

ACTIVITY 3: WHAT IF…?

Components: CQ Action, CQ Knowledge

Goal: Use improvisation to discover and build upon new ideas that cultivate curiosity.

Action plan:

- Spend the day thinking, *What if?*

- Play out the different scenarios in your mind.

- Journal or discuss them with a friend or colleague.

Perspective-taking questions:

- How will your life change if the scenarios come true?

- How can you share the scenarios with others?

ACTIVITY 4: I SPY…

Components: CQ Action, CQ Knowledge, CQ Drive

Goal: Stimulate curiosity by getting familiar with an impromptu object you see.

Action plan:

- Identify an object, then say, "I Spy with little eyes…"

- Google the object using "fun facts about [insert object name]."

- Share your findings with a friend or colleague.

Perspective-taking questions:

- What information surprised you the most about the object?

- What was your friend's or colleague's reaction?

ACTIVITY 5: FIVE MINUTES

Components: *CQ Action, CQ Knowledge*

Goal: Expand your worldview by incorporating different perspectives into your understanding.

Action plan:

- Pick a topic you know little about and spend five minutes reading about it.

- Find an opportunity to bring it up in conversation.

- The goal isn't to be an overnight expert but to add new dimensions to your understanding of the world. Plus, it may make for great conversation starters!

Perspective-taking questions:

- What surprised you the most?

- What preconceived notions did you have about the topic, and how have they changed after learning more?

Remember, being culturally curious is not a "one-and-done" thing. It's a lifelong journey. Start with these exercises to jump-start your quest for understanding and empathy. The world is rich and diverse. Each day presents a new opportunity to learn something extraordinary.

CHAPTER 17

Empathy

—

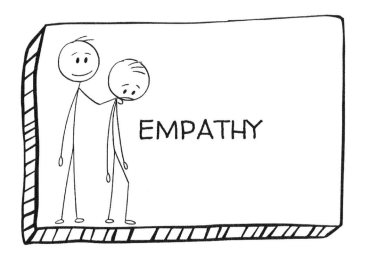

Could a greater miracle take place than for us to look
through each other's eye for an instant?
—*HENRY DAVID THOREAU*

"*Cancelalo!*" my father said to me.

"*Pero porque?*" I asked.

"*Te dije que eso está muy caro,*" he explained.

"*Pero por que no lo dejamos asi. Ya no tenemos opciones,*" I replied.

"*Te dije que lo canceles.*"

"Okay, Papi."

This was the first time my father asked me for help with a flight arrangement to return to the United States from the Dominican Republic. He wanted to return within a week, and it must be "*bueno, bonito, y barato*" (champagne with a beer budget). I needed to turn the impossible into a possibility. I stopped everything and started my search. After a few searches, I found the information and booked the least effective flight possible. When my father found out how much the flight cost, he asked me to cancel the flight reservation because he could find a cheaper option. Of course, I was fuming at this point. I tried reasoning with him to no avail. Begrudgingly, I agree to cancel the reservation once he finds a new one. Moments later, he asked me to leave the reservation as is because he could not find a cheaper option.

Once I overcame my ego, I wondered about navigating this new phase. A phase filled with humanity and empathy. One that I am not prepared for but committed to demonstrating the love my parents deserve from me. Navigating a relationship with an aging parent is complex and often emotionally fraught. For me, it's also an experience mired in cultural nuances that make it even more complicated. Then, I considered how the **C.H.O.I.C.E.** playbook helped me navigate this new phase of life.

I start with CQ Knowledge, digging into the cultural values that have shaped my father's life. He grew up in a very different time, with distinct expectations around family roles, aging, and independence. For him, admitting aging vulnerabilities might be perceived as a weakness. His pride and desire for independence are deeply rooted in the social norms he has lived through. Understanding this, I'm better equipped to sensitively approach discussions about his well-being without imposing my values and expectations.

I then use CQ Strategy to plan our discussions. Thinking about how best to communicate sensitive subjects like living situations or healthcare respects his dignity and autonomy. Instead of confrontation, I use a more nuanced approach. My CQ Drive helps me connect with "why." I want to understand and relate to my father. It motivates me to continually reach out, to be patient, and to strive for a meaningful connection, even when he becomes resistant or stubborn. This inner drive is powered by a genuine desire to know more about his life story, the experiences that have shaped him, and the wisdom he conveys. CQ Action helps me put it all together.

I turn all the understanding, strategy, and motivation into meaningful interaction. For example, recognizing that my father perceives direct offers of help as an affront to his independence, I might phrase things differently. Instead of saying, "Dad, I think you should do X," I might say, "What are your thoughts on X? I've heard it could be a good idea."

Recognizing I don't have all the answers, I summon cultural humility as the undercurrent that runs through all these efforts. I acknowledge that my cultural perspectives are just that—perspectives, not facts. I listen more than I speak. When I speak, I ask questions that help me understand his viewpoint better. My goal is not to "solve" the "problem" of my father's aging but to collaborate to create a life chapter that respects his wishes and dignity.

EMILY

What sets Emily apart is her empathy. If empathy were a currency, she would be a millionaire. Even while navigating the cultural minefield in the City of Love, Emily is an empathy queen. Antoine shows up with his wife, Catherine, at a Savoir event where Emily is tasked with protecting a two-million-dollar watch worn by Brooklyn, an American actress. Emily worries about how Silvie will feel when she sees Antoine with his wife. Despite Silvie's iceberg attitude toward her, Emily's unwavering concern for Silvie's feelings makes her an empathy queen supreme! Sylvie is like an ice sculpture—beautiful but cold. Emily could easily label her a "snob" and move on, but she doesn't. She listens, observes, and begins to understand the complexities of being Sylvie. Is she standoffish? Yes. But Emily picks up that this could be a defense mechanism or perhaps something that comes from the challenges of being a woman in a leadership role. Emily's ability to empathize earns her the grudging respect of her boss, and she starts to crack that ice-cold exterior (Fleming 2020).

When Emily meets Mindy, the ex-pat nanny, they immediately click. But their relationship isn't just surface-level chats about hot French guys and the best croissants in town (Fleming 2020).

Mindy went through a truly difficult time after facing technical issues during her performance on a TV show, which led to her father's identity being publicly discussed. It was a truly humiliating experience for her. She decided to leave everything behind and moved to Paris to study business. However, things didn't go as planned, and she had to quit school after her father cut her off financially. Mindy turned to being a nanny, teaching Mandarin to two children of a wealthy family to make ends meet. As Emily hears about Mindy's past, she listens with empathy, refraining from interrupting or offering hasty solutions. Rather than offering quick fixes, she genuinely validates Mindy's feelings, encouraging her to give her dreams of singing another shot. It's a moment that solidifies their friendship, as Emily reminds Mindy that life offers more than just one chance to find your groove (Fleming 2020).

In a nutshell, Emily's empathy is her secret sauce, her *je ne sais quoi*, her "it factor." Whether dealing with workplace dynamics, friendships, or messy romantic scenarios, her ability to put herself in other people's shoes makes her stand out. And let's be real, it's probably why we're all secretly—or not so secretly—rooting for her (Fleming 2020).

CARLOS

Carlos faces a delicate balancing act that many can relate to. Born to a Colombian family deeply rooted in traditional values, he's also a product of American society, which often leans toward individualism and personal ambition. He understands the tension between his family's traditional values and his personal goals is more than just a conflict. It's an intersection of different facets of his identity. Carlos confronts this tension directly, exhibiting an empathetic approach.

Empathy, for Carlos, goes beyond merely understanding or sharing another's feelings. It involves a nuanced appreciation of his family's cultural history. He recognizes the trust and collective decision-making his family values aren't simply traditions but have been formed through generations of lived experiences. These values serve as a compass, guiding relationships and offering a sense of community, which is particularly essential when navigating life in a new country.

Carlos also realizes that his aspirations—whether that's a career his family finds unconventional or lifestyle choices that diverge from tradition—are not rebellions but expressions of his complex identity. His empathetic insight doesn't pit his family's collectivism against his personal individualism. Instead, he seeks a dialogue between the two.

To foster this understanding, Carlos starts conversations with family members. These are not confrontational interactions but open dialogues where he lays out his thoughts, aspirations, and concerns while leaving room to hear theirs. He asks about their past, their dreams, and the compromises they've had to make, understanding their viewpoints are not merely opinions but life lessons. This isn't just a fact-finding mission. It's an empathetic exercise to create a shared understanding.

Carlos begins to reframe the concept of trust. He argues that trust can also mean believing in each individual's ability to make informed decisions, even if those choices are not the conventional path the family would expect. He reassures them that carving out his path doesn't equate to turning his back on family values. Instead, he's extending those values to include new forms of success and contentment.

Through these conversations, a transformation occurs within his family. They don't completely abandon their cherished values but become more open to integrating Carlos's perspectives into their collective worldview. It's a subtle but significant change that makes room for Carlos's pursuits and the family's core beliefs.

In exhibiting this level of empathy, Carlos accomplishes two important things: deepening his connection to his family's traditional values while making room for his identity to flourish. He deftly navigates the fragile equilibrium between honoring tradition and enabling personal growth, converting a potential point of conflict into an opportunity for collective evolution. Carlos's empathy thus serves as both a bridge and a compass, guiding him and his family through the complexities of identity in an ever-changing world.

GHITA

Originally from Morocco, Ghita immersed herself in New York City, where she now lives. Ghita goes beyond just respecting traditions. She actively listens to her neighbors, colleagues, and friends to understand their perspectives and challenges. Her empathetic approach enhances her coaching style, turning her into a bridge between differences. She recalls visiting a client in NYC from Paris, where she was based.

"It was time for lunch, and everyone was still sitting at their desk. I gathered everyone and invited them to lunch," she says, proving that empathy goes both ways. Ghita's empathy is reflected when she helps everyone around her feel genuinely heard and respected, cultivating a sense of inclusivity that benefits everyone. Ghita's empathetic nature teaches us how to create a sense of belonging no matter where you are.

CREATING MOMENTS THAT MATTER

Empathy, in its true essence, is about understanding and sharing the feelings of another. Let's craft experiential activities that blend your desired components and encourage people to cultivate this invaluable skill.

ACTIVITY 1: M.E.D.S. CHALLENGE

Components: *CQ Strategy, CQ Action*

Goal: Gain firsthand insights and deepen your understanding of self-care and its role in becoming culturally intelligent.

Action plan:

- Spend a week adjusting your sleep patterns to achieve six to seven hours of sleep.

- Remove five ultra-processed foods for a week, as much as you can.

- Spend a week staying present in all tasks. Even if you're taking out the garbage, stay present doing that.

- Incorporate one new ten-minute movement into your routine (walking, running, dancing, etc.).

Perspective-taking questions:

- How do you feel compared to before you implemented the changes?

- What specific changes did you notice in your physical and mental well-being?

- What challenges or roadblocks did you encounter in your self-care journey, and how can you overcome them?

ACTIVITY 2: CULTURAL EXCHANGE DINNERS

Components: *CQ Action, CQ Drive*

Goal: Engage senses and emotions through culinary experiences.

Action plan:

- Host or participate in monthly potluck dinners where each person brings a dish significant to their culture.

- Spend time discussing each dish's story.

Perspective-taking questions:

- How did tasting someone's culture change or affirm your perceptions about them?

- What emotions did a particular dish or its story evoke?

ACTIVITY 3: GLOBAL STORY EXCHANGES

Components: CQ Strategy, CQ Drive, Cultural Humility

Goal: Cultivate a narrative perspective of cultural empathy.

Action plan:

- Pair up with someone from a different cultural background (either online or offline.

- Exchange personal stories about a specific theme (e.g., childhood, festivals, challenges).

Perspective-taking questions:

- How does their story make you feel?

- What parallels can you draw between their story and your experiences?

ACTIVITY 4: ROLE EXCHANGE CULTURAL SCENARIOS

Components: *CQ Knowledge, CQ Strategy*

Goal: Sharpen your skills in understanding and empathizing with how people from different cultures might react in everyday situations. Dive into the nuances of how culture shapes behavior and emotion.

Action plan:

- Take on the role of a person from a different cultural background and simulate a common life event (e.g., a job interview or a family dinner). Have someone else play the role of another culture, or you could even switch roles halfway through.

Perspective-taking questions:

- How did you feel stepping into someone else's cultural shoes?

- Were there moments where you felt uncomfortable or unsure?

- What differences did you notice in how someone from culture A would handle the situation compared to someone from culture B?

- What do these differences tell you about what each culture values or considers important?

ACTIVITY 5: CULTURAL MEDITATION SESSIONS

Components: CQ Action, CQ Drive

Goal: Emotionally resonate with diverse cultures, forging deeper empathetic connections.

Action plan:

- Respectfully participate in meditation sessions incorporating elements from various cultures, like Tibetan singing bowls or Native American flute music.

Perspective-taking questions:

- What emotions or memories did the cultural elements invoke?

- How did the meditation deepen your emotional connection to that culture?

Empathy is a journey that demands both understanding and feeling. As you dive into these activities, let yourself be vulnerable and open to the emotions they might stir. The beauty of empathy lies in its ability to blur borders and create a shared human experience.

CHAPTER 18

Epilogue: A Milestone, Not a Finish Line

Do your little bit of good where you are; it is those little bits
of good put together that overwhelm the world.
—*ARCHBISHOP DESMOND TUTU*

"But you're supposed to know what this stuff is. You're the CQ psychologist," she said.

"I'm not an expert. I am a learner just like you," I replied.

My friend was surprised to hear about a recent CQ blunder I committed. I was telling her about the incident to highlight how the road to becoming culturally intelligent is a journey and not a destination. Just because I made a **C.H.O.I.C.E.** doesn't mean I am an expert. I am a learner.

EMILY

In season three, Emily's journey into Cultural Intelligence (CQ) evolves remarkably, taking her character into deeper, more nuanced explorations of diverse worldviews and complex social scenarios. Having laid the foundation of her understanding in the previous seasons, Emily is now seen actively applying her CQ skills in more challenging and high-stakes environments (Fleming 2020).

From enjoying a laid-back lunch by the Ferris wheel with Luc to balancing her support for Silvie in her new venture, her cultural intelligence is the compass that steers her in the right direction even when she is torn between two worlds (Fleming 2020).

Spoiler alert: The season starts with Emily taking on a role with Silvie's new marketing venture while she remains employed by Madeline at Savoir. Although this is a recipe for disaster that gets her fired again by Silvie, Emily's nuanced understanding of Madeline and Silvie's predicament earns her a CQ gold star. Thanks to her evolving CQ skills, she tackles this sensitive issue with grace, wisdom, and an uncanny ability to make people introspect. It's a powerful display of her evolved CQ skills, highlighting how she learns and applies her understanding in practical scenarios that yield success (Fleming 2020).

Here, we see her deftly navigate through a labyrinth of different power-distance challenges, communication styles, work ethics, and expectations. She employs her nuanced understanding of power dynamics to balance her loyalty to Silvie and Madeline, recognizing the different cultural imprints of both. The episodes focus on how Emily's knowledge of time orientation, value systems, and emotional expressions are invaluable assets. She is often the mediator, the bridge that connects different perspectives and fosters an environment of inclusivity.

Season three is also sprinkled with moments where Emily makes minor faux pas, like misunderstanding a cultural ritual or missing the context in an idiomatic expression. Still, these serve as reminders the journey to high CQ is ongoing. Emily sees each stumble as a lesson, an opportunity to grow, adding layers to her character that make her more relatable and human (Fleming 2020).

In season three, Emily articulates an entire French phrase to Gabriel's grandmother, surprising Gabriel. As the season wraps up, it's clear that Emily's CQ skills have evolved and become an integral part of who she is, both professionally and personally. Her journey has moved from theoretical understanding to real-world application, from learning to active practice, making her a powerful inclusion ally. And so, as Emily continues to weave through the rich tapestry of cultural experiences, she becomes a role model for how cultural intelligence can be a transformative force in our lives (Fleming 2020).

EVOLVING

It's been a few years since I found myself at that critical juncture, an intersection of identity and cultural awakening.

Time has a way of offering perspective, like viewing a landscape from a higher vantage point. The hills and valleys of my journey into cultural intelligence have softened, their edges less stark but no less significant.

It would be comforting to think of myself as fully evolved, a complete entity whose cultural awareness is all-encompassing and whose sensitivity knows no bounds. Yet, if there's one thing this journey has taught me, it's that complacency is the enemy of progress. The road to understanding our shared humanity is not a sprint but a marathon with no finish line.

The Cultural Intelligence Center, a springboard into this new chapter of my life, was just the beginning. The real work, I've found, happens in the mundane moments of day-to-day existence. It happens when we fall back into old thought patterns, dare to question our biases, and deliberately step out of our comfort zones.

Today, I work as a leadership development consultant and coach. I've channeled my passion for cultural intelligence into empowering others and helping organizations weave a cultural tapestry as vibrant as the communities they serve. Yet, each workshop, coaching session, and heartfelt conversation with someone whose experience is vastly different from mine serves as a teaching moment for them and a learning moment for me.

Surprisingly, my role as an educator in leadership development has been my most humbling experience yet. Every session I conduct reveals another layer of my ignorance, another area for personal growth. The challenge is never over.

It merely evolves, presenting new opportunities to push my boundaries and sharpen my understanding.

It's an ongoing battle to ensure that my work, our work, does not become a trendy buzzword or a checkmark on a corporate to-do list. There are still moments of awkwardness and instances where my good intentions don't quite bridge the gap of understanding. But these are the moments I now cherish. They're clear signs I am still learning, growing, and striving to improve. I am no expert by any means.

My journey into cultural intelligence has unexpectedly changed my relationships outside my professional life. Friends and family have noticed the shift, and many have joined me on this path. My family references the CQ language in daily dialogue. We quip about having "uncertainty avoidance" differences when making decisions.

Together, we've started forming a community within a community, a microcosm of the world we aspire to see—one where understanding trumps division, curiosity replaces judgment, and empathy heals the wounds of misunderstanding.

The stakes are high. As our world faces unprecedented social, political, and environmental challenges, the need for unity has never been more urgent. We must understand how to communicate, collaborate, and solve complex problems across various cultures, beliefs, and experiences. But even when the task scale feels overwhelming, I find hope in remembering that global change starts with individual actions.

In each thread of cultural understanding, I weave into the broader tapestry of my life, I see the reflection of countless others doing the same. Threads form patterns, patterns turn into tapestries, and tapestries join to become an unbreakable fabric of shared existence.

There's an old saying that a single step begins a journey of a thousand miles. When I first stood at the crossroads of self-discovery and cultural awakening, I took that first step—not knowing where it would lead yet understanding its necessity.

Today, I still stand at a crossroads of sorts. With every decision to act, speak, listen, and learn, I take another step down the path of cultural intelligence. And although the path ahead remains unclear, shrouded in complexities and challenges, the journey has become my destination.

As I close this book, literally and metaphorically, I'm filled not with a sense of completion but with a spirit of anticipation. The page turns, and a new chapter beckons—one of continual growth, endless learning, and the pursuit of a more compassionate world.

The miracle of our shared human journey isn't just about arriving somewhere. It's about the wisdom we gain along the way, the lives we touch, and the world we shape through our collective actions. It's a dance between understanding and being understood, a play of light and shadow that molds our human experience. What once felt like an identity crisis now appears as a mosaic of possibilities, a stepping stone on a path that promises self-discovery and the actualization of a shared vision for humanity.

As I venture into this new chapter, my eyes are wide open, eager to soak in more perspectives, cultural nuances, and wisdom. I no longer see differences as barriers but as bridges, not as wedges but as weaves in a tapestry of endless complexity and beauty. And I realize this tapestry connects us all, forming a quilt that provides warmth in the cold, comfort in the unknown, and unity in diversity.

So, let's keep weaving, let's keep learning, and most of all, let's keep growing! The tapestry is far from complete. Each thread we add enriches it, each color we introduce enlivens it, and each pattern we incorporate beautifies it. As we pull the threads of understanding tighter, we come closer to the aspiration that has fueled this journey all along: a world woven tightly together not by sameness but by a rich complexity that celebrates every thread, every color, every unique design.

Let's carry this vision with us as we each turn our pages, knowing that the book is never truly closed, the journey never really done, and the tapestry is always awaiting another vibrant thread. And that, my friends, is the joy and the responsibility of living in our incredibly diverse, endlessly fascinating, and profoundly interconnected world.

Come along.

Learn.

Explore.

Learn some more.

Adapt without adopting.

Make the **C.H.O.I.C.E.** today!

With love and appreciation,

Loren

Contact me:
Loren Rosario-Maldonado
pr@lorenrosario.com
www.lorenrosario.com

RESOURCES

———

WEBSITES

1. Cultural Intelligence Center: https://culturalq.com.

2. CQ and Cultural Values Assessment: https://culturalq.com/products-services/assessments.

3. Deliberate Directions: https://www.deliberatedirections.com.

4. Hofstede Insights: https://www.hofstede-insights.com.

5. US Census Bureau: https://www.census.gov.

RESEARCH

House, Robert J., Paul J. Hanges, Mansour Javidan, Peter W. Dorfman, and Vipin Gupta. 2004. *Culture, Leadership, and Organizations: The GLOBE Study of 62 Societies.* Thousand Oaks: SAGE Publications.

- Provides a fully integrated narrative featuring contributions from various experts that form a cohesive exploration of the theory underlying the GLOBE program, which is distinctive for its cross-cultural design, collaborative research methodology, and comprehensive data collection.

Ang, Soon, and Linn Van Dyne. 2015. *Handbook of Cultural Intelligence: Theory, Measurement, and Applications.* New York: Routledge.

- Provides a comprehensive overview of the current scientific understanding of cultural intelligence and its importance in managing diversity, both intra-culturally and inter-culturally. Unlike traditional texts that focus on comparing and describing cultures through national norms, beliefs, and customs, this handbook prioritizes individual capabilities. It highlights the traits that enable individuals to operate successfully in diverse cultural environments, underscoring that these skills can be cultivated through education and experience.

BOOKS

Abrams, Hesha. 2022. *Holding the Calm: The Secret to Resolving Conflict and Defusing Tension.* Oakland: Berrett-Koehler Publishers.

- A guide to handling conflict and defusing tension most effectively.

Burchard, Brendon. 2022. *High Performance Habits: How Extraordinary People Become That Way.* Carlsbad: Hay House, Inc.

<bulllets1>A guide to building long lasting habits that are aligned with your values and yield maximum impact while building character and integrity.

Cabral, Amber. 2022. *Say More About That: …And Other Ways to Speak Up, Push Back, and Advocate for Yourself and Others.* Hoboken: John Wiley & Sons.

- The book provides a comprehensive guide to communication strategies for championing equity, which you can use to advocate for others.

Grant, Adam. 2021. *Think Again: The Power of Knowing What You Don't Know.* New York: Viking.

- A book about learning, unlearning, and relearning through curiosity rather than judgment.

Kahneman, Daniel. 2011. *Thinking, Fast and Slow.* UK: Penguin.

- Kahneman sheds light on the reliability and limitations of our intuitions and how to harness the advantages of deliberate thought.

Livermore, David A. 2009. *Cultural Intelligence: Improving Your CQ to Engage Our Multicultural World.* Baker Academic.

- Examines the essential competency of cultural intelligence (CQ) and the capacity to function efficiently across various national, ethnic, and organizational cultures.

Livermore, David, and Soon Ang. 2015. *Leading with Cultural Intelligence: The Real Secret to Success.* New York: AMACOM.

- This updated version of *Leading with Cultural Intelligence* equips you to succeed in any business setting, whether internationally or locally.

Livermore, David. 2022. *Digital, Diverse & Divided: How to Talk to Racists, Compete with Robots, and Overcome Polarization.* Oakland: Berrett-Koehler Publishers.

- Provides insight into managing challenging discussions with anyone.

Meyer, Eryn 2014. *The Culture Map (INTL ED): Decoding How People Think, Lead, and Get Things Done Across Cultures.* Hachette: Public Affairs.

- This book navigates us through this nuanced and potentially hazardous landscape where individuals from vastly different backgrounds are anticipated to collaborate smoothly. Meyer offers a proven model for understanding how cultural variances affect global business, blending a thoughtful, analytical structure with practical, hands-on recommendations.

Nyamwaya, Lyna. 2022. *Leading with Cultural Humility: 12 Inclusive Practices to Manage Biases. Promote Equity,*

Inclusion, and Belonging. Minneapolis: Bold Impact Group LLC.

- Helps navigate real-life challenges, manage biases, improve communication, and cultivate inclusion.

Schein, Edgar H. 2013. *Humble Inquiry: The Gentle Art of Asking Instead of Telling.* Oakland: National Geographic Books.

- Expands and enriches the idea of humble inquiry, viewing it not merely as a method for asking questions but as a comprehensive approach that encompasses improved listening, more effective responses to what others are attempting to communicate, and greater self-disclosure.

Zilberglait, Miriam, MD, FACP. 2003. *The 3G Cycle of Life: The Secrets for Achieving Joy, Meaning, and Well-Being.* 2023. New Degree Press.

- A book about well-being, burnout, and their impact on mental health and leadership development.

Acknowledgments

In this labor of love, I have been blessed with a village of unwavering supporters, all of whom I wish to name here.

First and foremost, I want to extend my deepest and most heartfelt gratitude to God, the author of my life and the source of all inspiration. It is by Your grace alone this endeavor has been made possible. You have given me the opportunity, wisdom, and strength to complete this work. I am eternally thankful. Through each challenge and victory, Your presence has been a constant guide, a reminder that no task is impossible when fortified by faith. Thank you for the gift of creativity, the community (angels) that has supported me, and the incredible chance to amplify my voice through this book. May it serve as a testament to Your boundless love and endless opportunities for those who seek to do Your will.

To Mami y Papi, who provided the foundational values upon which this work stands. To Robert, the cornerstone of my life, your unconditional love and encouragement have been my sanctuary and an emotional anchor that sustained me through the late nights and endless revisions. To my daughter

Sarah, who is a force to be reckoned with and pushes me to be my best every day. To David Livermore, whose mentorship, wisdom, and friendship have become my North Star. Thank you for accepting the invitation to be interviewed!

I am forever grateful to my CQ Fellowship cohort, Marc, Trisha, Rick, Carol, and Sula, Kristal, Jennifer, Mike, Kristin, Allison, Amber, Lucy, Margaret, Marisa, Rahn, Tara, and Tim, for your collective wisdom.

To my CHIEF Core 1,000 group, Liz, Laura, Tiffany, Helen, Lauren, Christine, Christina, and Adrienne, whose support I can always count on. Your formidable force is priceless!

To my supporters who, without you, this book would never have been published.

To those of you who summoned the courage to share your story here: Kiera, Sarah, Ayesha, Laura, Alex, Sam, Jack, Lisa, John, Maria Jose, Susan, Andrew, Lina, Ben, Richard, Nina, Sophia, George, Jessica, Chen, Jennifer, James, Mark, Raj, Martha, Mei, Miguel, Jonas, Jake, Eugina, Mirna, Sofie, Rihab, Enrique, Gary, Carlos, and Ghita—I am eternally grateful!

To my mentors and advisors, your unwavering encouragement has been my fuel. Most significantly, to Carolyn J. Ortega, PsyD, this seed would have never been planted without your support and unwavering encouragement during that multicultural class all those years ago! To Angel Alexander Flores, whose mentorship led to the career of my dreams.

To our girls at Girls Inc. of Greater Miami, whose future is more promising than our past.

To Virginia Akar, your sisterhood and unwavering support mean more to me than you'll ever know.

To my brilliant Manuscripts LLC editor, Frances Chiu, who saw potential in every scribbled line and prose, thank you for believing in this project as much as I did.

To my family and friends, who offered endless therapy supplies, humor, tequila, and perspective—thank you for being my haven! Sarah, Ashley, Miriam, Lucy, Tasha, Ghita, Rihab, and Eugina, thank you for the space for endless Loren'sms and for never giving up on me!

Thanks to my VIP readers, Sarah Maldonado, Virginia Akar, Heidi Perloff, Helenmarie Blake, and Adriana Zabarain, whose early feedback has been invaluable.

Thank you, Manuscripts LLC, for helping me realize this dream and creating a community of unwavering support.

To you, the reader, for allowing me the privilege to share my thoughts and occupy a small space in your life. I hope this book brings you a fraction of the joy, insight, and fulfillment that writing it has brought me. Thank you all from the bottom of my heart.

Finally, special thanks to everyone who supported my presale campaign to make this book possible:

Abel Rosario
Allison Coventry
Ardeshir Mehran
Ashley Valentin
Ayanna Edwards
Berkys Mejia
Carlos Castillo
Carlos Maldonado
Carol Bunch Davis
Christian Pedroza
Cristina Frias
Cynthia Mota
Eric Koester
Ernesto Tejeda
Eugina Jordan
Frances Jeanette Rosario
German Dilone
Ghita Filali
Gina Ghura
Heidi Perloff
Helenemarie Blake
Iris Rodriguez
Jennet James
Jennie Byrne
Johnny Rosario
Juan and Claritza Maldonado
Katherine William-Botrous
Katty Medina
Kenia Rincon
Kiko Ochoa
Kinga Vajda
Laura Juanes Micas
Laura Perez

Lauren Brunswick
Lisa DeConto
Lisa Vasquez-Fedrizzi
Liz Papasakelariou
Lucy Chen
Mabelyn Rosario
Marc Geil
Martin Bonner
Maureen Presinal
Melva Midi
Mercedes Maldonado
Monica Brown
Nalby Intharaksa
Natalia Maldonado
Natasha Durkins
Nithasha Yakoob
Nur Lakhani
Omaira Rivas
Rafaela Guzman
Rihab Babiker
Sacha Seraydarian
Sarah Maldonado
Sayi Neufeld
Steven Ashley
Sunilbe Siceron
Talar Coursey
Tiersa Smith-Hall
Tiffany Compress
Virginia Akar
Yisel Fernandez
Yohi Popiol

APPENDIX: CITATIONS

INTRODUCTION

Earley, P. Christopher, and Soon Ang. 2003. *Cultural Intelligence: Individual Interactions Across Cultures*. Stanford: Stanford University Press.

Livermore, David A. 2009. *Cultural Intelligence: Improving Your CQ to Engage Our Multicultural World*. Grand Rapids: Baker Academic. E-book Format.

Livermore, David. 2011. *The Cultural Intelligence Difference: Master the One Skill You Can't Do Without in Today's Global Economy*. New York: Harper Collins Leadership. E-book Format.

CHAPTER 1—WHO ARE *YOU*?

Livermore, David A. 2009. *Cultural Intelligence: Improving Your CQ to Engage Our Multicultural World*. Grand Rapids: Baker Academic. E-book Format.

CHAPTER 2—WHAT *EMILY IN PARIS* LEARNS ABOUT CQ

Fleming, Andrew. 2020. *Emily in Paris.* Darren Star Productions; Jax Media MTV, Entertainment Studios, 2020-23 https://www.netflix.com/search?q=Emily%20in%20Paris&jbv=81037371.

Goleman, Daniel. 2007. *Social Intelligence.* New York: Random House. E-book Format.

Goleman, Daniel. 1995. *Emotional Intelligence.* New York: Bantam Dell. E-book Format.

Livermore, David A. 2009. *Cultural Intelligence: Improving Your CQ to Engage Our Multicultural World.* Grand Rapids: Baker Academic. E-book Format.

Livermore, David. 2011. *The Cultural Intelligence Difference: Master the One Skill You Can't Do Without in Today's Global Economy.* New York: Harper Collins Leadership. E-book Format.

CHAPTER 3—LOOKING IN THE MIRROR

Fleming, Andrew. 2020. *Emily in Paris.* Darren Star Productions; Jax Media MTV, Entertainment Studios, 2020–23 https://www.netflix.com/search?q=Emily%20in%20Paris&jbv=81037371.

Rogers, C. 1959. "A theory of therapy, personality, and interpersonal relationships as developed in the client-centered framework." In (ed.) S. Koch, *Psychology: A study of a science. Vol. 3: Formulations of the person and the social context.* New York: McGraw Hill.

Sharma, Robin. 2011. *The Greatness Guide*. Toronto: HarperCollins Publishers. E-book Format.

Trompenaars, Fons, and Peter Woolliams. 2003. *Business Across Cultures*. West Sussex: Capstone Publishing Ltd (a Wiley Company). E-book Format.

CHAPTER 4—CULTURAL VALUES DEMYSTIFIED

Fleming, Andrew. 2020. *Emily in Paris*. Darren Star Productions; Jax Media MTV, Entertainment Studios, 2020-23 https://www.netflix.com/search?q=Emily%20in%20Paris&jbv=81037371.

Livermore, David. 2011. *The Cultural Intelligence Difference: Master the One Skill You Can't Do Without in Today's Global Economy*. New York: Harper Collins Leadership. E-book Format.

Livermore, David A. 2009. *Cultural Intelligence: Improving Your CQ to Engage Our Multicultural World*. Grand Rapids: Baker Academic. E-book Format.

CHAPTER 5—A WORLD BEYOND WORDS

Bullock, Barbara E., and Almeida Jacqueline Toribio. "Reconsidering Dominican Spanish: data from the rural Cibao." *Revista Internacional de Lingüística Iberoamericana* (2009): 49–73.

Fleming, Andrew. 2020. *Emily in Paris*. Darren Star Productions; Jax Media MTV, Entertainment Studios, 2020–23 https://www.netflix.com/search?q=Emily%20in%20Paris&jbv=81037371.

Hall, Edward T. 1973. *The Silent Language.* New York: Anchor Books.

Hall, Edward T. 1977. *Beyond Culture.* New York: Anchor Books.

CHAPTER 6—TIME, TIME, TIME

Fleming, Andrew. 2020. *Emily in Paris.* Darren Star Productions; Jax Media MTV, Entertainment Studios, 2020-23 https://www.netflix.com/search?q=Emily%20in%20Paris&jbv=81037371.

Hall, Edward T. 1977. *Beyond Culture.* New York: Anchor Books.

Hofstede, Geert, Gert Jan Hofstede, and Michael Minkov. 2010. *Cultures and Organizations: Software of the Mind, Third Edition.* USA: McGraw Hill Professional. E-book Format.

Trompenaars, Fons, and Peter Woolliams. *Business Across Cultures.* West Sussex: Capstone Publishing Ltd (a Wiley Company), 2004). E-book Format.

CHAPTER 7—JUST TELL ME WHAT TO DO

Hofstede, Geert, Gert Jan Hofstede, and Michael Minkov. 2010. *Cultures and Organizations: Software of the Mind, Third Edition.* USA: McGraw Hill Professional. E-book Format.

CHAPTER 8—IS TRUST UNIVERSAL?

Hofstede, Geert, Gert Jan Hofstede, and Michael Minkov. 2010. *Cultures and Organizations: Software of the Mind, Third Edition*. USA: McGraw Hill Professional. E-book Format.

Van Dyne, Linn, Don Vandewalle, Tatiana Kostova, Michael E. Latham, and L. L. Cummings. "Collectivism, propensity to trust and self-esteem as predictors of organizational citizenship in a non-work setting." *Journal of Organizational Behavior* 21, no. 1 (2000): 3–23.

CHAPTER 9—WHY CAN'T WE JUST GET ALONG

Fleming, Andrew. 2020. *Emily in Paris*. Darren Star Productions; Jax Media MTV, Entertainment Studios, 2020–2023. https://www.netflix.com/search?q=Emily%20in%20Paris&jbv=81037371.

Hofstede, Geert, Gert Jan Hofstede, and Michael Minkov. 2010. *Cultures and Organizations: Software of the Mind, Third Edition*. USA: McGraw Hill Professional. E-book Format.

CHAPTER 10—KNOWLEDGE IS POWER

"About Tostones." ifood.tv (blog), n.d., https://ifood.tv/south-american/tostones/about.

Clara, Tia. 2023. "Kipes or Quipes (Dominican Kibbeh)." *Dominican Cooking* (blog). July. https://www.dominicancooking.com/kipes-quipes-dominican-recipe.

El Cocinero Puerto-Riqueño o Formulario Para Confeccionar Toda Clase de Alimentos, Dulces y Pasteles Conforme a Los Precefitos de La Química y La Higiene y a Las Circunstancias Especiales Del Clima y de Las Costumbres Puerto-Riqueñas. 1859.

Empar. 2020. "The Spanish Arroz Con Leche." *United Planet* (blog). November 9, 2020. https://www.unitedplanet.org/blog/2009/06/02/the-spanish-arroz-con-leche.

Livermore, David A. 2009. *Cultural Intelligence: Improving Your CQ to Engage Our Multicultural World.* Grand Rapids: Baker Academic. E-book Format.

Livermore, David. 2011. *The Cultural Intelligence Difference: Master the One Skill You Can't Do Without in Today's Global Economy.* New York: Harper Collins Leadership. E-book Format.

Mufarech, Antonia. 2022. "A Brief History of Puerto Rico's Beloved Mofongo." Smithsonian Magazine, April 20, 2022. https://www.smithsonianmag.com/travel/a-brief-history-of-puerto-ricos-beloved-mofongo-180979947.

Nakada, Makoto, and Takanori Tamura. 2005. "Japanese Conceptions of Privacy: An Intercultural Perspective." *Ethics and Information Technology* 7 (1): 27–36. https://doi.org/10.1007/s10676-005-0453-1.

CHAPTER 11—C.H.O.I.C.E. PLAYBOOK

Hook, Joshua N., Don E. Davis, Jesse Owen, Everett L. Worthington, and Shawn O. Utsey. 2013. "Cultural Humility: Measuring Openness to Culturally Diverse Clients." Journal of Counseling Psychology 60 (3): 353–66. https://doi.org/10.1037/a0032595.

Van Dyne, Linn, Soon Ang, Kok Yee Ng, Thomas Rockstuhl, Mei Tan, and Christine Koh. 2012. "Sub-Dimensions of the Four Factor Model of Cultural Intelligence: Expanding the Conceptualization and Measurement of Cultural Intelligence." *Social and Personality Psychology Compass* 6 (4): 295–313. https://doi.org/10.1111/j.1751-9004.2012.00429.x.

Tervalon, Melanie, and Jann Murray-García. 1998. "Cultural Humility versus Cultural Competence: A Critical Distinction in Defining Physician Training Outcomes in Multicultural Education." *Journal of Health Care for the Poor and Underserved* 9 (2): 117–25. https://doi.org/10.1353/hpu.2010.0233.

CHAPTER 12—COURAGE

Fleming, Andrew. 2020. *Emily in Paris.* Darren Star Productions; Jax Media MTV, Entertainment Studios, 2020–23 https://www.netflix.com/search?q=Emily%20in%20Paris&jbv=81037371.

CHAPTER 13—HUMILITY

Fleming, Andrew. 2020. *Emily in Paris*. Darren Star Productions; Jax Media MTV, Entertainment Studios, 2020–23 https://www. netflix.com/search?q=Emily%20in%20Paris&jbv=81037371.

CHAPTER 14—OPENNESS

Fleming, Andrew. 2020. *Emily in Paris*. Darren Star Productions; Jax Media MTV, Entertainment Studios, 2020–23 https://www. netflix.com/search?q=Emily%20in%20Paris&jbv=81037371.

CHAPTER 15—INTEGRATION

Fleming, Andrew. 2020. *Emily in Paris*. Darren Star Productions; Jax Media MTV, Entertainment Studios, 2020–23 https://www. netflix.com/search?q=Emily%20in%20Paris&jbv=81037371.

CHAPTER 16—CURIOSITY

Fleming, Andrew. 2020. *Emily in Paris*. Darren Star Productions; Jax Media MTV, Entertainment Studios, 2020–23 https://www. netflix.com/search?q=Emily%20in%20Paris&jbv=81037371.

CHAPTER 17—EMPATHY

Fleming, Andrew. 2020. *Emily in Paris*. Darren Star Productions; Jax Media MTV, Entertainment Studios, 2020–23 https://www.netflix.com/search?q=Emily%20in%20Paris&jbv=81037371.

Printed in Great Britain
by Amazon